Panorama of the city.

THE CITY

In the case of a city like Florence it is difficult, when writing about her, to resist the temptation of treating her as a great museum, full of exceptional objects isolated in a glass case. Yet in Florence, as everywhere else, monuments, churches, palaces and sculpture are all related, have a common evolution, live and talk to us, communicating history, anecdotes, ideas. In view of this, the present book has been conceived as an attempt to give a voice to things that have been objects of passive admiration, silent and enigmatic too long; to seek out their history, the circumstances and people that brought them into connection, not overlooking small but significant episodes or facts. Above all not idealising one artist or work of art to the detriment of others, or placing periods that are wrongly considered "minor" too far beneath the "major" ones.

Recent excavations in Piazza della Signoria. Facing page: detail of the fresco by *Vasari* in Palazzo Vecchio, depicting **"Florence during the siege of 1530"**.

HISTORY

The origins of Florence go back to the Etruscan epoch, when Fiesole dominated the valley from its hill. Groups of inhabitants went down to the banks of the Arno to found a village, modest, but destined to thrive, thanks to its favourable position on the direct line of communication between the north and south of Italy; although this did make it more vulnerable by enemy attack and invasion. The Romans soon founded a colony here with the auspicious name of Florentia (that is, destined to flourish). Already in the 2nd century B.C. the new municipality had acquired a position of pre-eminence among the cities of the Roman *Tuscia*. The town survived the Dark Ages to emerge slowly in the Carolingian epoch. First the feud of the Marquises of Tuscany, among whom Ugo and Matilda should be recorded, from the 11th century onwards Florence began to acquire greater and greater autonomy; in 1115, after the struggles against the simoniacal clergy and the feudal lords of the surrounding neighbourhood, the Florentine Comune had virtually come into being; ten years later the new state defeated her rival, Fiesole. Soon, inside the city, now surrounded by a new circle of

walls, the first clashes began to take place between immigrant overlords and the artisan class, organised into the extremely powerful Guilds and Trade Corporations. These clashes created the two factions of the Guelphs (who supported the Pope) and the Ghibellines (who favoured the Emperor) with the distinct prevalence of the former. After the end of the 13th century the Guelphs themselves divided into two parties of "black" and "white", which had split up on the basis of a long-standing rivalry; the black party, supported by the Pope, sent the white partisans into exile in 1303; these included Dante Alighieri. In the meantime Florence was becoming more powerful, fighting against rival cities (Pistoia, Arezzo, Volterra, Siena) and expanding her territory. Also in the cultural and economic fields, at the turn of the 13th-14th century she was becoming, one of the most important centres in Italy. This was the period of the great companies of bankers and merchants, when the wool and silk industries were flourishing. In 1348 there was a terrible outbreak of plague, described by Boccaccio at the beginning of the *Decameron*. The last decades of the 14th century saw

Costantino Guerra

FLORENCE

All the Art Treasures of the City

400 color photographs

City map

BONECHI EDIZIONI "IL TURISMO"

INDEX

Reprint 2005

© Copyright by Bonechi Edizioni "Il Turismo" S.r.l
Via G. Di Vittorio, 31 - 50145 Florence - Italy
Tel. +39-055.37.57.39 / 34.24.527
Fax +39-055.37.47.01
e-mail: info@bonechionline.com
        bbonechi@dada.it
Internet: http://www.bonechionline.com
Printed in Italy

Photos: Bonechi Edizioni "Il Turismo" S.r.l. Archives; Marco Rabatti;
Rolando Fusi; Giuliano Valsecchi (K&B News): page 118 (bottom) and
page 119; Nicola Grifoni
Photolitography: Studio Leonardo, Florence
Print: Lito Terrazzi, Firenze
ISBN 88-7204-050-7

5

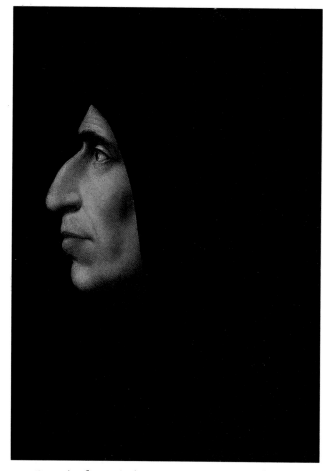

Portrait of Fra Girolamo Savonarola, by *Fra Bartolomeo* (Museum of San Marco).

After Cosimo his son Francesco I acceded to the government of the city; a lover of art and letters, he had little propensity for ruling. The following century saw the beginning of the city's decline; international factors (the preponderance in Europe of the great powers of France, Austria and Spain; the shift northwards of the centres of economic power) and the lack of significant personalities among the Medici Grand Dukes, with the exception of Ferdinando II, all combined to exclude Florence, as for that matter the whole of Italy, from the category of European powers. The extinction of the dynasty with Gian Gastone (1737) and the passing of the Grand Duchy to the Lorraine family, connected with the ruling Austrian house, allowed Florence to recover a certain marginal importance in Europe. The Lorraines ruled the Grand Duchy, except during the period of Napoleonic domination (1799-1814), until the union of Florence and Tuscany with Italy (1859). Florence was the capital of the new kingdom from 1865 to 1871. The city continued to be, as it is now, a lively artistic and cultural centre. It suffered grave damage in World War II, and during the 1966 flood, remedied by intense and careful restoration.

PAINTING

In the 13th century all the artists working in Florence underwent the influence of Byzantine art. The decoration of the Cupola of the Baptistry, which belongs to this period, was executed by Roman and Venetian workers; certainly the contact these had with local elements contributed to the formation of a Florentine school, whose greatest representative was Cimabue (1240-1304). He too seems to have worked on the Baptistry mosaics, but he managed to elude the Byzantine influence and bring a more realistic conception to bear on his painting. However his attempts at reform would have been vain had he not found, in his pupil Giotto di Bondone, a painter who furthered his ideas and who is to be considered the true pioneer of Florentine painting. Giotto (1267-1337), assimilated the teaching of Cimabue and of the Roman school of Cavallini to free himself completely of the Byzantine influence and create a realistic style, of powerful humanity, with a volumetric conception of masses and an incisive, harmonious rhythm of line: among his masterpieces are the *Maestà* (Majesty) in the Uffizi and the frescoes in Santa Croce. A large group of painters underwent Giotto's influence; among the followers nearest to the master, Maso di Banco, the painter of the frescoes in the Bardi di Vernio Chapel in Santa Croce, and Taddeo Gaddi, (c. 1300-66) who reveals, in the frescoes of the Baroncelli Chapel, also in Santa Croce, the influence of the Sienese school, whose greatest exponents were Duccio di Buoninsegna, (c. 1255-1318), active in Florence around 1285, Pietro Lorenzetti (c. 1280-1348), Ambrogio Lorenzetti (died 1348) and Simone Martini (c. 1285-1344). Florentine artists in whom the influence of Giotto merged with that of the Sienese school were Bernardo Daddi (c. 1290-c. 1348), Nardo di Cione and his brother Orcagna (1308-68: Strozzi Chapel in Santa Maria Novella). At the beginning of the 15th century Florence predominated in painting with Lorenzo Monaco (1370-1425: *Adoration of the Magi* at the Uffizi) and Masolino da Panicale (1348-

increasingly violent clashes between the *popolo grasso*, the rich middle class which ruled the state by means of the Guilds, and the *popolo minuto* or working-class. The struggle came to a head in the *Tumulto dei Ciompi* (humble carders in the Wool Guild) by means of which the lower classes of the citizenry came to power (1378). But soon afterwards the oligarchy headed by the Albizi regained the ascendancy by supporting the small populace; the rich Medici family was acquiring increasing political importance, and soon the rule of the Signoria was established, although republican appearances were preserved. Cosimo the Elder, who founded the Medici rule, was succeeded by Lorenzo the Magnificent, a shrewd statesman and a great patron of the arts. The century that culminated in the rule of the Magnificent (died 1492) is one of the most brilliant in Florentine history, especially in the field of culture and art; it was the century of Humanism and the great art of the Renaissance. Between the end of the 15th and the early 16th century the city had a free Republican government, after the expulsion of Piero, the successor to Lorenzo. This period is dominated by the figure of Girolamo Savonarola. After the Medicis returned, Florence remained under their rule until 1527, when a fresh revolt restored the Republican institutions. But the Medicis, supported by the Emperor and the Pope, returned once more after a harsh siege (1530). Despite the political unrest, the years between the end of the 15th century and the first decades of the 16th century were rich in great personalities in the artistic and literary fields (Michelangelo, Machiavelli, Guicciardini). In 1569 Cosimo dei Medici, the ruler of the city, received the title of Grand Duke, which he passed on to his successors.

View of the Old Market with the column of Abundance, by *G. Moricci,* 1860 (Museo di Firenze com'era).

1425: works in the Brancacci chapel at the Carmine church). These artists brought a reflection of International Gothic into Florentine painting, until Masaccio (1401-28/29) freed himself from Gothic trappings and returned to the direct simplicity and plastic solidity of Giotto, having also assimilated the plastic conquests of

Donatello and those of Brunelleschi in the field of perspective. His greatest masterpiece is the cycle of frescoes in the Brancacci Chapel, in the church of the Carmine. The new style of Masaccio influenced almost all the painters of the period, beginning with the master himself, Masolino da Panicale. Paolo Uccello (1397-

1475) followed in his footsteps in the study of perspective (frescoes in the Green Cloister in Santa Maria Novella, *Battle of San Romano* at the Uffizi) while Andrea del Castagno (1423-57: *Last Supper* at Sant'Apollonia) developed the plasticity of the figure. At the same time Fra Angelico (c. 1378-1455) merged the sense of form inherited from Masaccio with his own particular kind of spirituality (Museum of San Marco). Filippo Lippi (1406-69) was formed by Fra Angelico, speaking, however, a blunter language; his pupil and assistant was Benozzo Gozzoli (1420-97: chapel of Palazzo Medici Riccardi). Artists of the second half of the 15th century are Antonio del Pollaiolo (1432-98: Uffizi Gallery) Verrocchio (1435-88: *Baptism of Christ* at the Uffizi) who had Leonardo in his workshop; Domenico Ghirlandaio (1449-94) the jolly teller of sacred stories (church of Santa Maria Novella and Sassetti Chapel in Santa Trinita); Sandro Botticelli (1445-1510), the pupil of Lippi, formed on the manner of Verrocchio and Pollaiolo, but an isolated creator of his own, peculiarly Florentine style, highly rhythmical in line and very lyrical; then Filippo Lippi, (c. 1457-1504), the companion and disciple of Botticelli. At the end of the 15th and the beginning of the 16th century appear the masterpieces of the great Leonardo da Vinci (1452-1519), the creator of a new mysterious chiaroscuro (works at the Uffizi), of Michelangelo Buonarroti (1475-1564): *Doni Tondo* at the Uffizi, and of Raphael (1483-1520: works at the Uffizi Gallery and Palatine Gallery). Andrea del Sarto (1486-1530) revealed a very personal treatment of form and colour (church of the Santissima Annunziata, Uffizi Gallery); his followers were Jacopo Pontormo (1494-1556: *Descent from the Cross* in Santa Felicita), Rosso Fiorentino (1494-1540) and Franciabigio (1482-1525). All these painters adhered to a style based on the models of Michelangelo and Raphael, which was later known as Mannerism; Agnolo Allori, called Bronzino, (1503-72) and Giorgio Vasari (1511-74) also belonged to this current. Cigoli, Poppi and Empoli were active at the turn of the 16th and 17th century, and in the 17th century Matteo Rosselli (1578-1650), Francesco Furini (c. 1600-1646) and Giovanni da San Giovanni (1592-1636), a skilled interior designer (Silver Museum and Palazzo Pitti). Florentine painting had no particular vitality in the following period, until the revolutionary movement of the Macchiaioli grew up, after 1850; after the neo-classical movement in the early 19th century, led by Pietro Benvenuti, and the reaction back to classicism on the part of Giuseppe Bezzuoli, Antonio Ciseri and Stefano Ussi. The Macchiaioli artists were so called because they sought to render reality by means of the *macchia* or blob of colour, with the details of figures and objects implied, so to speak. The characteristics of this type of painting in a certain sense anticipate those of the French Impressionists. The first Macchiaioli group included Giovanni Fattori (1825-1908), Silvestro Lega (1826-95), and Telemaco Signorini (1825-1901). Macchiaioli and post-Macchiaioli works are exhibited in the Gallery of Modern Art in the Pitti Palace. Avant-garde currents in painting in this century (Cubism and Futurism) were represented in Florence by Ardengo Soffici and Ottone Rosai.

Two paintings by *Piero della Francesca*. Left: **Portrait of Battista Sforza**. Right: **Portrait of Federico da Montefeltro** (Uffizi Gallery)

SCULPTURE

No real school of sculpture existed in Florence in the Romanesque period, while at Pisa Nicola Pisano had already given the art a new life. At the beginning of the Gothic period, Arnolfo di Cambio was working in Florence as a pupil and collaborator of Nicola Pisano (c. 1232-1302) who introduced Pisan motifs in the sculptures for the façade of the Cathedral (now in the Cathedral Museum). Giotto, who was the architect of the Bell-tower, also designed and executed part of the sculptured decoration of the building, but the true founder of the Florentine school of sculpture was Andrea da Pontedera, called Andrea Pisano (1290-1349). In 1330 he began the doors of the Baptistry in Florence and in 1337 succeeded Giotto in the construction of the Bell-tower, decorating it with bas-reliefs which are among the finest sculptures of the century (the designs are attributed to Giotto). Another great sculptor was Andrea di Cione called Orcagna, who was also a painter, architect and poet; his masterpiece is the tabernacle at the church of Orsanmichele. At the beginning of the 15th century Lorenzo Ghiberti (1378-1455) achieved the outstanding creation of the Baptistry door, called the "Door of Paradise". The central figure, however, of this period was Donato de' Bardi called Donatello (c. 1386-1466) who revolutionised sculpture, infusing his works with greater naturalism and a keener historical sense; new, also, was his interpretation of the bas-relief in the characteristic "flattened" style, with very low relief. The followers of Donatello were Rossellino, Benedetto da Maiano (1442-97) and Luca della Robbia (c. 1400-82) who worked mainly in glazed terracotta. Luca's artistic heirs were his nephew Andrea della Robbia (1435-1528) and Andrea's five sons, of whom the most important is Giovanni (1469-1529). Two outstanding sculptors of the mid-16th century were Andrea di Cione called Verrocchio and Antonio del Pollaiolo. This century is dominated by the figure of Michelangelo Buonarroti whose works influenced all the sculptors of the following period. Among those in Florence who most felt this influence were Baccio Bandinelli (1488-1560) and Bartolomeo Ammannati (1511-92: the *Neptune* of the fountain in Piazza della Signoria). A singular 16th century artist was Benvenuto Cellini (1500-71); a goldsmith first and foremost, he brought to sculpture the precision of his craft (*Perseus*, Loggia della Signoria). Another great Renaissance sculptor was Giambologna, born in Flanders but Italian by adoption (1524-1608), who shows the influence of Michelangelo but reveals a strong personality of his own (*the Rape of the Sabine women*, Loggia della Signoria). In the 17th and 18th centuries the exponents of Florentine sculpture were disciples of Giambologna: Pietro Tacca (1577-1640) and Giovan Battista Caccini (1556-1613). In the 19th century the greatest representative of the Tuscan school was Lorenzo Bartolini (1777-1850) who contested the new Mannerism derived from Canova, for a return to the study of nature.

David, by *Donatello* (National Museum of the Bargello).

Examples of various architectural styles - From top to bottom and left to right: *Etruscan gate; Roman arch of triumph; Romanesque portal; two-light window in Gothic style; Renaissance architecture; Baroque window; large Art Nouveau window; contemporary architecture.*
On the facing page: **the dome of the Cathedral.**

ARCHITECTURE

The contribution of Florence to the Romanesque style in the 11th century can be seen in the Baptistry, San Miniato al Monte and the church of Santi Apostoli. About halfway through the 13th century the Cistercians brought with them the Gothic style. This was the epoch of Arnolfo di Cambio, the greatest Italian architect of the period who began the construction of Santa Maria del Fiore, Palazzo della Signoria, Santa Croce and Orsanmichele. The pioneer of Renaissance architecture was Filippo Brunelleschi(1377-1446) who reacted against the Gothic influence, creating his own personal style, classical yet new, and combining pietra serena with plaster in harmonious simplicity (the old Sacristy of San Lorenzo, the Hospital of the Holy Innocents, Pazzi Chapel, Pitti Palace and the Cupola of the Cathedral). Michelozzo Michelozzi (1392-1472) was a pupil of Brunelleschi; his most important works are Palazzo Medici and the monastery of San Marco. Other contemporary or later architects who underwent Brunelleschi's influence and returned to the forms of classical architecture, were Giuliano da Sangallo (1445-1516: Santa Maria Maddalena dei Pazzi); Simone del Pollaiolo called Cronaca (1457-1508: San Salvatore al Monte); Giuliano da Maiano (1432-90, Palazzo Pazzi); Benedetto da Maiano (Palazzo Strozzi). Leon Battista Alberti (1404-72) broke away from Brunelleschi; a humanist, man of letters, poet, painter, sculptor and author of scientific treatises, his masterpieces are Palazzo Rucellai and the façade of Santa Maria Novella. In the 16th century the Brunelleschi tradition broke off, and Baccio d'Agnolo (1462-1543) created a new type of lordly mansion that was continued throughout the century (Palazzo Guadagni, Palazzo Bartolini-Salimbeni and the bell-tower of Santo Spirito). Antonio da Sangallo the Elder (c. 1455-1534) was intensely active as a military and civil architect. Michelangelo Buonarroti returned to the classic Florentine style, faithful to Brunelleschi in the play of pietra serena on plaster, with the New Sacristy of San Lorenzo, and the Laurentian Library. Meanwhile Giorgio Vasari was building the Uffizi and adapting the interior of Palazzo Vecchio. The Baroque style had few exponents in Florence: Matteo Nigetti (c. 1560-1649: the façades of San Gaetano and of Ognissanti) and Ferdinando Ruggieri (façade of San Firenze). Later, in the 19th century, an attempt was made to return to traditional classical motifs in architecture; the architect Giuseppe Poggi (1811-1901) created Piazzale Michelangelo and transformed the outer zone of the city. The rebuilding of the façades of the Cathedral and of Santa Croce in the neo-Gothic style also took place in the nineteenth century. In the present century the light and floral "liberty" style appeared in Florence in the villas designed by Giovanni Michelazzi (1876-1920). This was followed by the rationalist architecture of Pier Luigi Nervi (Football Stadium) and of Giovanni Michelucci (railway station of Santa Maria Novella and the church of St. John the Baptist on the Autostrada del Sole motorway).

THE MEDICI FAMILY
Genealogical Tree

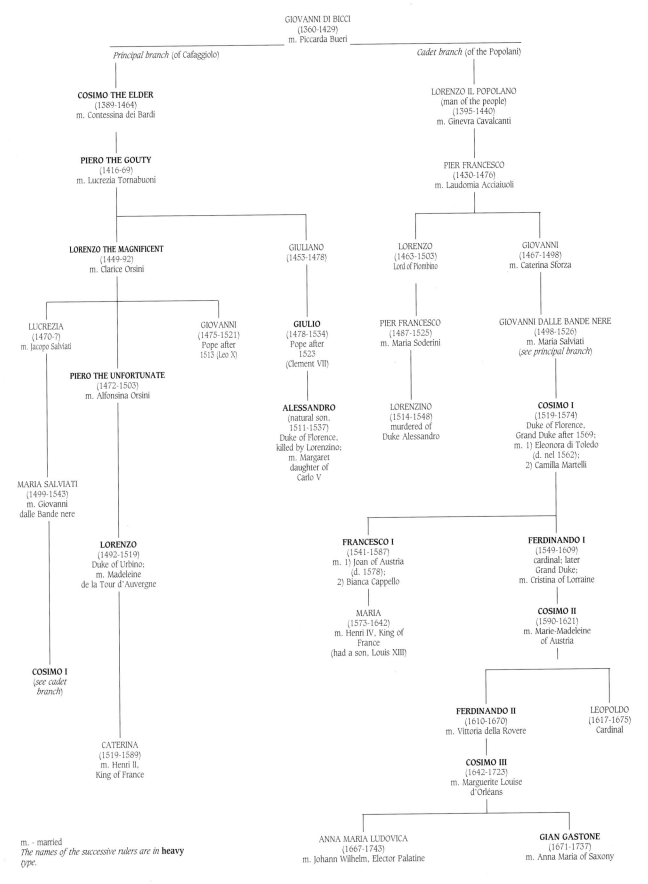

GIOVANNI DI BICCI
(1360-1429)
m. Piccarda Bueri

Principal branch (of Cafaggiolo)

Cadet branch (of the Popolani)

COSIMO THE ELDER
(1389-1464)
m. Contessina dei Bardi

LORENZO IL POPOLANO
(man of the people)
(1395-1440)
m. Ginevra Cavalcanti

PIERO THE GOUTY
(1416-69)
m. Lucrezia Tornabuoni

PIER FRANCESCO
(1430-1476)
m. Laudomia Acciaiuoli

LORENZO THE MAGNIFICENT
(1449-92)
m. Clarice Orsini

GIULIANO
(1453-1478)

LORENZO
(1463-1503)
Lord of Piombino

GIOVANNI
(1467-1498)
m. Caterina Sforza

LUCREZIA
(1470-?)
m. Jacopo Salviati

GIOVANNI
(1475-1521)
Pope after
1513 (Leo X)

GIULIO
(1478-1534)
Pope after
1523
(Clement VII)

PIER FRANCESCO
(1487-1525)
m. Maria Soderini

GIOVANNI DALLE BANDE NERE
(1498-1526)
m. Maria Salviati
(*see principal branch*)

PIERO THE UNFORTUNATE
(1472-1503)
m. Alfonsina Orsini

ALESSANDRO
(natural son,
1511-1537)
Duke of Florence,
killed by Lorenzino;
m. Margaret
daughter of
Carlo V

LORENZINO
(1514-1548)
murdered of
Duke Alessandro

COSIMO I
(1519-1574)
Duke of Florence,
Grand Duke after 1569;
m. 1) Eleonora di Toledo
(d. nel 1562);
2) Camilla Martelli

MARIA SALVIATI
(1499-1543)
m. Giovanni
dalle Bande nere

LORENZO
(1492-1519)
Duke of Urbino;
m. Madeleine
de la Tour d'Auvergne

FRANCESCO I
(1541-1587)
m. 1) Joan of Austria
(d. 1578);
2) Bianca Cappello

FERDINANDO I
(1549-1609)
cardinal; later
Grand Duke;
m. Cristina of Lorraine

MARIA
(1573-1642)
m. Henri IV, King of
France
(had a son, Louis XIII)

COSIMO II
(1590-1621)
m. Marie-Madeleine
of Austria

COSIMO I
(*see cadet
branch*)

FERDINANDO II
(1610-1670)
m. Vittoria della Rovere

LEOPOLDO
(1617-1675)
Cardinal

CATERINA
(1519-1589)
m. Henri II,
King of France

COSIMO III
(1642-1723)
m. Marguerite Louise
d'Orléans

ANNA MARIA LUDOVICA
(1667-1743)
m. Johann Wilhelm, Elector Palatine

GIAN GASTONE
(1671-1737)
m. Anna Maria of Saxony

m. - married
The names of the successive rulers are in **heavy**
type.

The **coat of arms** of the family that governed Florence for three centuries (1434-1743) was a certain number of red balls (varying from 6 to 9) on a gold ground: the exact significance of this coat of arms is not known. After 1466, by concession of King Louis XI, one ball could bear the lilies of France.

Giovanni Averardo, known as Bicci, the founder of the Medici family fortunes. From his marriage to Piccarda Bueri, he had Cosimo, who was the head of the "Cafaggiolo" branch of the family and Lorenzo, who became the head of the "Popolani" branch. Giovanni di Bicci was the first Medici to subsidise the arts in a way that was to give the family lasting fame in Florence and in history.

Cosimo the Elder, the rich representative of a dynasty of merchants, became so powerful in the first half of the 15th century, and created such envy, that he was sent into exile. Recalled in 1434, he was elected Standard-Bearer and led the Medici family to power.

Giuliano, the son of Piero, known as the Gouty, and brother to Lorenzo de' Medici. One of his youthful loves was Fioretta Gorini, who gave him a son, Giulio. He was killed at the early age of 25 on the 26th April 1478 in the Cathedral of Florence during the bloody brawl of the Pazzi Plot.

Giulio, son of Giuliano, became the second Medici pope, assuming the name of **Clement VII**. His reign coincided with the most heated period of the Franco-Spanish war; he was confronted by the enmity of the powerful Colonna family and had to take refuge several times in Castel Sant'Angelo. After the Sack of Rome, he had to oppose Henry VIII of England, which brought about the schism of the Church of England. He died in 1534.

Lorenzo the Magnificent, the grandson of Cosimo, took over the rule of Florence in 1469. An absolute governor, he was an able man of letters, the patron of artists and philosophers and a shrewd diplomat; under his government Florence became the greatest cultural centre in Europe.

Piero, the Magnificent Lorenzo's firstborn son, was totally unlike his father in having no interest in culture, art or politics. In 1494, he proved incapable of confronting the King of France Charles VIII's troops and was forced to flee the town, together with his younger brethren. He died in exile in 1503, a failure, who had seen his family achieve renown and success, without in the least understanding what had gone into creating them.

Giovanni, the son of Lorenzo the Magnificent, became Pope under the name of **Leo X** in 1513, after becoming a cardinal at the age of 13, but a priest only after he had been elected pope. He was the patron of Raphael and Bramante, the Lutheran schism took place during his reign (1571).

Cosimo I was the son of the condottiere Giovanni dalle Bande Nere, and of Maria Salviati, grand-daughter of Lorenzo the Magnificent. An able statesman at the head of a strong army, he transformed Tuscany into a Medici state: he was the first to assume the title of Grand Duke (1569).

Eleonora di Toledo, daughter of the vice roy of Naples, was the first wife of Cosimo I, who restored a wing of Palazzo Vecchio for her use and bought the Pitti Palace for the family: together, they patronised many artists: Vasari, Ammannati, Cellini, Bronzino, Giambologna.

Francesco I, the son of Cosimo, succeeded his father as ruler of the State. Reserved by nature, he was more interested in art, and in alchemy, than in government. His second wife was Bianca Cappello, his former mistress: they both died in 1587 in the villa of Poggio a Caiano within a few hours of each other.

Ferdinand Ist, the son of Cosimo Ist. An intelligent, wise ruler, he had a strong sense of family dignity. He tried to resume contacts with France and in 1587 married Christine of Lorraine. He restructured many buildings and sponsored the inlaid semi-precious stone laboratories. He died in 1609. His rule can be considered the highest point of the Grand Ducal period.

The Cathedral and Giotto's Bell Tower.

PIAZZA DEL DUOMO

At the dawn of the Middle Ages, the site of the Piazza was a mass of dwelling houses and public buildings. The church of Santa Reparata was built over the foundations of one of these latter in the 4th century. Three centuries later (though some think in the same century) the Baptistry was erected next to the church, and this place began to form the centre of religious life in Florence. Santa Reparata became a cathedral in 1128. The church was becoming too small for this new role and greater dignity— the population was increasing too – and in 1289 the Comune decided to enlarge it. This was part of an extensive rebuilding plan that involved the widening out of the city walls (the Roman circle was too small), the construction of a Priors' Palace (now Palazzo Vecchio) and alterations to existing buildings such as Santa Croce, the church of the Badia, Orsan-michele, the Bargello and the Baptistry. In order to achieve a city that should be new but harmonious, one man, Arnolfo di Cambio, was given the responsibility of directing and coordinating the work. One of the greatest architects and sculptors of his time, he raised the level of the piazza (which he had re-paved), eliminating the podium on which the Baptistry previously stood, demolished a few houses nearby, and began to build the new cathedral, for which he planned a cupola and external decoration matching that of the Baptistry. The death of Arnolfo in 1302 put a stop to the work, which was resumed in 1332-34 with the construction of the Bell-Tower under the direction of Giotto. The addition of a cupola by Brunelleschi (1420-36) made it the impressive, dominating building that we see today (the façade is a 19th century work).

The Baptistry of San Giovanni.

BAPTISTRY

Dante's "Bel San Giovanni", the religious building most beloved by the Florentines, was perhaps started in the 7th century, but the work done in the 11th-12th centuries made it the most important monument of Romanesque architecture in Florence. Its regular octagonal form and the symmetrical distribution of the external decoration were for centuries an architectural ideal for artists of the stature of Arnolfo, Giotto, Brunelleschi, Leon Battista Alberti, Leonardo and Michelangelo. It has three magnificent bronze doors. The South Door is the work of Andrea Pisano (c. 1330); it consists of 28 panels illustrating the *Life of the Baptist*; the bronze cornice is the work of Vittorio Ghiberti (son of Lorenzo, 1452). The North Door is by Lorenzo Ghiberti, executed 1403-1424, after winning a competition against Brunelleschi; the 28 panels represent epi-

sodes from the *Life of Christ*. The East Door, the famous "door of Paradise", is also by Lorenzo Ghiberti (1425-1452); it is composed of 10 gilt panels, with complex *Scenes from the Old Testament*, crowded with figures. The smooth pyramidal roof-covering is topped by a lantern. The inside of the Baptistry, like the outside, is on an octagonal plan with marble panelling and each wall divided into three by tall columns; the two-lighted windows of the women's gallery open above the trabeation. A baptismal font, mentioned by Dante in the *Divine Comedy*, used to stand in the centre of the very fine inlaid marble floor; this was removed in the 16th century by Buontalenti, by order of the Grand Duke Francesco I. Against the wall are a baptismal font of the Pisan school, 14th century; the tomb of the anti-Pope John XXIII, the work of Donatello and Miche-

The Door of Paradise, by *Lorenzo Ghiberti.*

Creation of Adam and Eve. – Original Sin. – Expulsion from Paradise.	Adam and Eve, Cain and Abel. – Abel keeping sheep and Cain ploughing. – Cain kills Abel. – Curse of Cain.
Story of Noah: Noah's family leaves the ark after the Flood. – Noah gives thanks to the Lord who sends a rainbow as a sign of peace. – Drunkenness of Noah. – Noah is derided by Ham and covered up by Shem and Japhet.	Story of Abraham: Sarah at the entrance to the tent. – Apparition of the angels to Abraham. – Abraham and Isaac on the mountain. – The Angel stays Abraham's hand as he is about to sacrifice Isaac.
Story of Jacob and Esau: Esau trades his birthright for a plate of lentils. – Isaac sends Esau hunting. – Jacob throws a goat's skin around his neck. – Isaac mistakes Jacob for Esau and gives him his blessing. – Jacob leaves his father's house.	Story of Joseph: Joseph is sold to the merchants and brought before Pharaoh. – Interpretation of Pharaoh's dream. – The golden cup in Benjamin's bag. – Joseph reveals himself to his brothers and forgives them. – Joseph meets Jacob.
Lorenzo Ghiberti	**Vittorio Ghiberti**
Story of Moses: Moses receives the Tablets of the Law on Mount Sinai. – Aaron waits halfway down the mountain. – The Hebrews, terrified by the thunder and lightning, await Moses' return at the foot of the mountain.	Story of Joshua: Joshua and the Hebrews cross the Jordan and crowd before the Ark. – The Hebrews gather twelve stones for commemoration. – The walls of Jericho fall at the sound of the Angels' trumpets.
Story of Saul and David: Saul defeats the Philistines. – David smites Goliath. – David carries Goliath's head before the cheering crowd, back to Jerusalem.	King Solomon ceremoniously receives the Queen of Sheba in the Temple of Jerusalem.

The East Door, the famous "Door of Paradise", as Michelangelo called it, was sculpted by Lorenzo Ghiberti between 1425 and 1452 with the help of his sons Vittorio and Tommaso, Benozzo Gozzoli and Michelozzo. The Guild of Merchants financed the work, commissioning Ghiberti to make the door "in the way he wanted, so that it would be the richest, most ornate, finest, most perfect that could be imagined; he was to spare neither time nor money to make it outdo and excel his other works". Of the twenty-seven years it took to complete the work, sixteen were devoted to chiselling after the casting. Ghiberti worked in full Renaissance spirit, abandoning the Gothic style of the North Door to adopt a measured, elegant form of naturalism, inherited from Brunelleschi and Donatello. Two porphyry columns stand on either side of the door: they were a gift from the citizens of Pisa to the Florentines as thanks for supplying military aid in 1117; the columns were split, probably during a flood, but the malicious Florentines said that they were already broken when they arrived and that they had been covered with a cloth to conceal the damage. This episode gave rise to the motto: "Florentines blind and Pisans treacherous".

Panels of the Door of Paradise – Above, from the left: **The Battle with the Philistines** and **King Solomon receiving the Queen of Sheba in the Temple**. Below: **Moses receiving the Tables of the Law on Mt. Sinai** (detail).

lozzo, commissioned by the banker Giovanni dei Medici, two Roman sarcophagi and a 13th century altar. The beautiful and very striking wooden statue of the *Magdalen* by Donatello (1435-55), which used to be in the Baptistry, is now on view in the Cathedral Museum. The internal sections of the cupola are covered by mosaics executed between the mid-13th and the mid-14th century by local and Venetian craftsmen (in the Middle Ages Venice was the greatest centre for mosaics). The most important artists who made the cartoons for the mosaics include Cimabue (*Scenes from the life of Joseph*) and Coppo di Marcovaldo (*Christ*). The subjects of the magnificent design are *Scenes from the Old and New Testament* and the *Last Judgment*, dominated by the impressive figure of the *Judging Christ*, more than twenty six feet high.

Scenes from the life of Joseph (detail). Below: **Scenes from the life of Joshua** (detail).

At the side: **the North Door,** by *Ghiberti* (1403-1424).

Scenes from the Life of Christ are depicted; above is a 16th-century work by Francesco Rustici: St John the Baptist Preaching.

Below: **the interior of the Baptistry.**

The vault of the Tribune is covered with 13th-century mosaics, the work of Fra Jacopo, called della Scarsella after this part of the Baptistry which forms a rectangular projection on the exterior. The monolithic columns set against the walls, some of oriental granite and others of cipolin, were recovered when other buildings were dismantled. There is a splendid floor in inlaid marble, black, white, red and green. Near the Paradise Door is a large slab, placed there by Strozzo Strozzi in the 11th century, that represents the Ptolemaic cosmic system with the sun and the signs of the Zodiac.

Preceding page: **the South Door**, by *Andrea Pisano* (14th century).

Episodes from the Life of the Baptist are depicted; above the door is the Martyrdom of St. John, by Vincenzo Danti (16th century).

The interior of the cupola of the Baptistry.

The 13th and 14th-century mosaics that cover the cupola of the Baptistry are by artists of the Venetian and Florentine schools; the decoration, on a gold ground, is divided into concentric bands. In the centre, round the opening of the lantern, are ornamental motifs; there follows the image of Christ surrounded by Seraphs and the angelic hosts, in the third band are scenes from Genesis (from the Creation to the Flood), in the fourth, the story of Joseph, in the fifth, scenes of the Life of Christ and in the last, the life of the Baptist. The apsidal zone is dominated by the colossal figure of Christ: on either side, in three superimposed bands, are: Angels announcing judgment; the Virgin, the Baptist and Apostles; the Resurrection of the Dead and the division of the Blessed and the Damned, with a terrible representation of Hell.

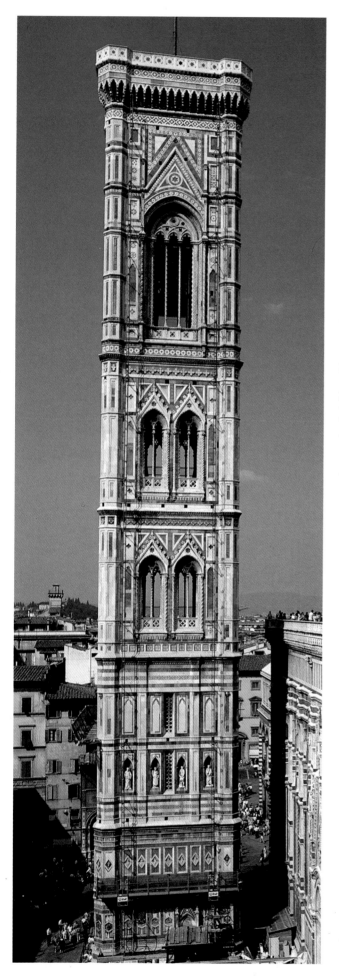

GIOTTO'S BELL TOWER

The building of this tower began in 1334 under the direction of Giotto, after a fire had destroyed the old bell-tower of Santa Reparata. Giotto died in 1337, when the base of the tower had been completed; after him work was directed by Andrea Pisano and Francesco Talenti, who brought it to conclusion (although the original plan included a spire which was never built). The building is of remarkable grace and elegance; the structure lightens and lengthens as it rises, becoming complex with marble insets and fine perforation. The bas-reliefs on the base (the originals are in the Cathedral Museum) were executed by Andrea Pisano and his workmen under the supervision of Giotto.

LOGGIA DEL BIGALLO

This was built between 1352 and 1358 by Alberto Arnoldi in elegant Gothic style. The front, facing the Baptistry, has three tabernacles with the statues of *St. Peter the Martyr*, the *Virgin and Child* and *St. Luke*. Inside is a fine collection of works of art, with frescoes detached from the building and works by Ghirlandaio, Arnoldi and the schools of Botticelli and Verrocchio.

Left: **Giotto's Bell Tower**. Below: **the Loggia del Bigallo**. Facing page: **the facade of the Cathedral**.

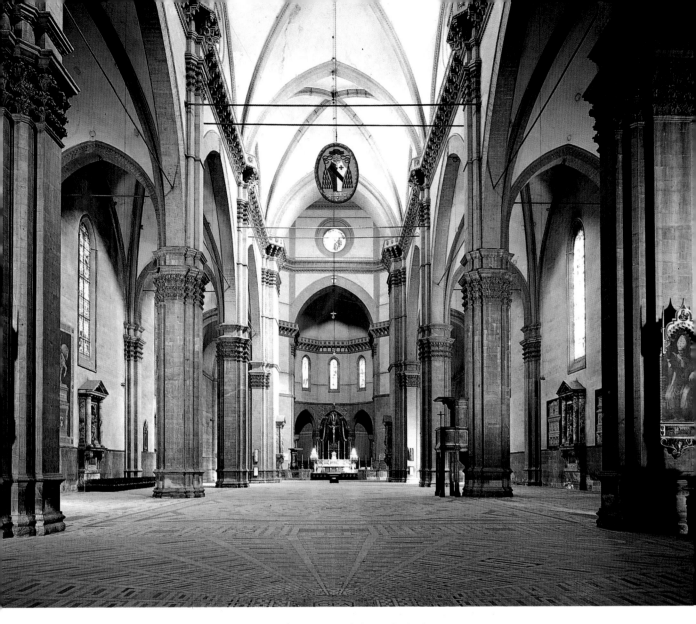

The interior of the Cathedral.

CATHEDRAL

The construction of the Cathedral, dedicated to Santa Maria del Fiore (St. Mary of the Flower) was begun in 1294 by Arnolfo di Cambio, chosen by the city authorities and the citizens, who wanted a cathedral not only larger than the previous church of Santa Reparata but also "so sumptuous and magnificent" that it would outdo the cathedrals of rival Tuscan cities both in beauty and dimensions. The new cathedral was erected round the older church, whose simple structure and two bell-towers were incorporated. Santa Reparata was finally pulled down in 1375; but the Florentines went on calling the new cathedral by the old name for a long time — the authorities had to inflict heavy fines in order to enforce the use of the new one, Santa Maria del Fiore. The lower part of Santa Reparata, buried underneath the floor of the Duomo till quite recently, can now be visited by going down a staircase from the right aisle; it contains remains of frescoes, sculptures and tombstones, including that of Filippo Brunelleschi. The

inside of the Duomo, solemn, spacious and light, was the scene of the fiery sermons of Savonarola, and of the savage Pazzi conspiracy. On April 26th 1478 members of the Pazzi family, enemies of the Medicis, in league with Archbishop Salviati, attacked Lorenzo the Magnificent and his brother Giuliano during Mass. Lorenzo escaped, but Giuliano was killed and the conspiracy was followed by harsh repression. Works of art of many centuries embellish the cathedral but do not alter the severity of its high ogival arches and composite pillars. On the inside of the façade is an enormous clock, executed in 1443 and decorated with four heads of *Prophets* painted by Paolo Uccello. Also by Paolo Uccello is the fresco of the *Monument to Giovanni Acuto* (John Hawkwood) on the wall in the left aisle; beside it is that of the *Monument to Niccolò da Tolentino*, by Andrea del Castagno (1456). Above the large octagonal tribune is the cupola by Brunelleschi. A competition for the construction of the cupola was

Two other views of the interior of the Cathedral.

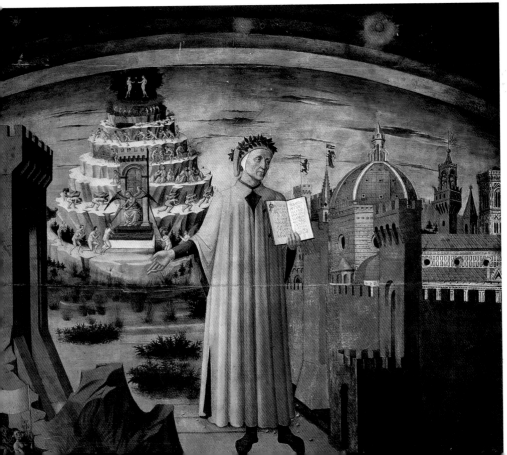

Above, left: **Monument to Niccolo' da Tolentino,** by *Andrea del Castagno.*

Niccolò da Tolentino was the captain of the city troops at the Battle of San Romano (1432).

Above: **Monument to Giovanni Acuto (John Hawkwood),** by *Paolo Uccello.*

John Hawkwod was an English condottiere appointed by the Republic to lead the Florentine militia from 1377 to 1394.

At the side: **Dante and the Divine Comedy,** by *Domenico di Michelino (1465).*

The painting, in the fourth bay of the left aisle of the Cathedral, depicts Inferno or Hell, Purgatory and Paradise and a view of contemporary Florence.

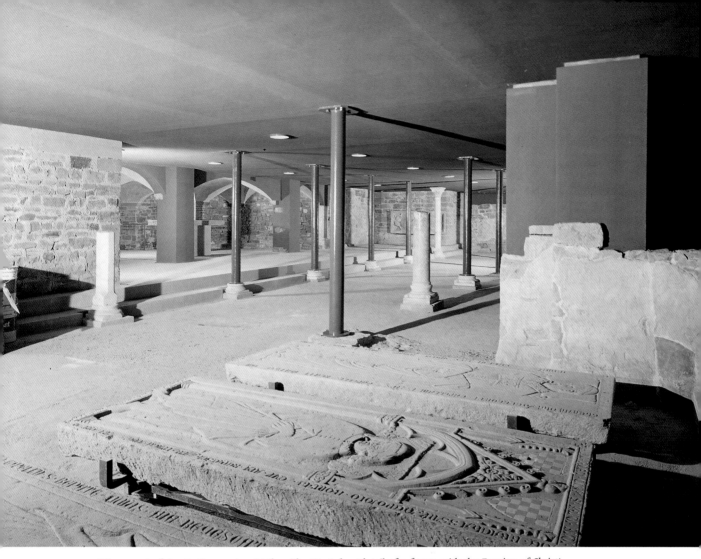

The crypt of Santa Reparata. At the side: **St. John** (detail of a fresco with the Passion of Christ).

announced in 1418. The difficulty of this task was immediately evident, for traditional building techniques were inadequate. Brunelleschi invented an original system of mobile centres which superseded the usual one of fixed structures starting from the ground (clearly impossible to use owing to the enormous dimensions of the building) and so succeeded in defeating Lorenzo Ghiberti, his eternal rival, who also took part in the competition. The cupola was closed up as far as the lantern in 1436. It is based on a massive octagonal drum, has marble ribbing and is covered by red tiles baked in the kilns at Impruneta. The inside of the cupola is decorated with frescoes by Giorgio Vasari and Federico Zuccari (1572-79) representing the *Last Judgment* in five superimposed bands. Over the high altar is a wooden *Crucifix* by Benedetto da Maiano; and round it is the octagonal choir by Baccio Bandinelli (1555), decorated with bas-reliefs. Behind the altar on the right is the Old Sacristy with an *Ascension* in terracotta by Luca della Robbia in the lunette over the entrance. Directly opposite on the other side of the Tribune is the New Sacristy, with a fine bronze door by Luca della Robbia, Michelozzo and Maso di Bartolomeo. In the lunette, *Resurrection*, also by Luca. Inside the sacristy, splendid 15th century inlaid cupboards. In the chapel at the end of the apse is a bronze urn by Ghiberti with relics of Saint Zanobius.

Above: two works by *Arnolfo di Cambio*. Left: **Madonna and Child**; right: **statue of Boniface VIII**. At the side: **the silver cross of the altar in the Baptistry**, by *Betto di Francesco, Antonio del Pollaiolo* and *Bernardino Cennini*.

CATHEDRAL MUSEUM

This museum contains works from the Cathedral, the Bell-Tower and Baptistry. A room on the ground floor houses the sculptures from the first façade of the Cathedral, demolished in 1587, with a splendid *Virgin and Child* by Arnolfo di Cambio. The next room contains building material and mechanical devices used by Brunelleschi when building the Cupola. Another small room has a collection of precious reliquaries. The famous *Pietà* by Michelangelo is on the mezzanine. On the floor above, the two choir-galleries by Donatello and Luca della Robbia; *panels* by Andrea Pisano from the Bell-Tower, the statues of *John the Baptist*, the *Magdalen* and *Habakkuk* by Donatello, and the silver altar from the Baptistry, the work of several artists including Michelozzo, Verrocchio and Pollaiolo.

The Room of the Choir-galleries. Below: **Choir-gallery**, by *Luca della Robbia* (details).

Above: **Choir-gallery**, by *Luca della Robbia* (detail).

Like the other, by Donatello, it was executed for the choir of the Cathedral and was placed over the door of one of the sacristies. Both were replaced by a larger wooden structure in 1686. In the ten panels, clearly delineated by the pilasters and brackets, Luca illustrated a psalm of David (quoted in the trabeation of the gallery), exhorting us to praise God with dance and song. The scenes express the master's typical serene composed classicism, with soft smooth forms.

At the side: **Saint Reparata**, by *Arnolfo di Cambio.*

Two works by *Donatello:* **Jeremiah** (above)
and **Habakkuk** (below) .

The Magdalen, a wooden statue, by *Donatello.*

Above, left: **The Blacksmith's Craft**. Above: **The Drunkenness of Noah.** At the side: **Grammar.**

These are three of the original panels which decorated Giotto's Bell Tower (now replaced by copies), executed by Andrea Pisano and helpers under the supervision of Giotto.

Facing page: **The Pietà**, by *Michelangelo (1553).*

This work, one of the master's last, was in the Cathedral for a long time, but was originally sculpted by the artist for his tomb in Santa Maria Maggiore in Rome, a project that was never terminated. This is perhaps the most dramatic of Michelangelo's versions of the Pietà: Christ's lifeless body sinks down at the centre of the pyramid formed by the three figures supporting it: the Magdalen, on the left, with an expression of calm sorrow given her by Tiberio Calcagni (the pupil who finished the work after the master's death); the sorrowing Nicodemus, whose face according to Vasari is a self portrait of Michelangelo; Mary, her expressive power enhanced by the fact that she is rough-hewn in Michelangelo's characteristic "unfinished" manner.

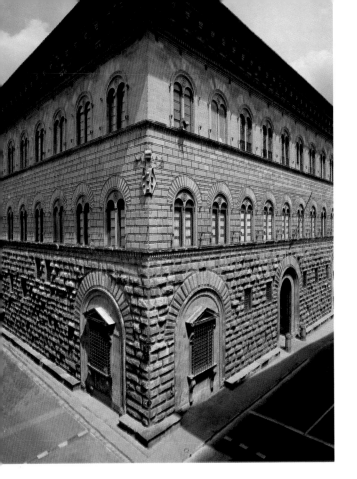

PALAZZO MEDICI - RICCARDI

Built for Cosimo the Elder in Via Larga, now Via Cavour, between 1444 and 1460, by the Florentine architect and sculptor Michelozzo Michelozzi, this was the prototype of all Florentine palaces of the Renaissance. Majestic and elegant, it was filled with works of art commissioned by the Medicis; the main branch of the family lived there until 1540. In 1655 the palace was sold to the Riccardi family and is now the seat of the provincial administration and the Prefettura. Exhibitions and other cultural events often take place here. It was designed by Michelozzo as a large cube, and must have stood out among the lower buildings round it; but the Riccardi family had it enlarged, adding seven new windows on Via Larga. The two principal sides, carefully designed by the architect with a view to the pictorial effect of the volumes, have pronounced rustication on the ground floor, flatter rustication on the storey above and smooth stones on the third. This motif was to reappear frequently for more than a century, along with the use of two-lighted windows with round arches. There is a fine classical cornice, while the big corner windows (called "kneeling windows" from the form of the corbels) which took the place of a previously existing loggia, are attributed to Michelangelo (c. 1517). On the same corner is a large Medici coat of arms, which, according to Benvenuto Cellini, was originally brightly coloured; seven red balls on a gold ground. Inside the palace is a

The facade of Palazzo Medici-Riccardi. Below: view of *Michelozzo's* courtyard in the palace.

The Journey of the Three Kings to Bethlehem, by *Benozzo Gozzoli* (detail). At the side: **the Chapel of Palazzo Medici Riccardi;** the **Nativity**, on the altar, is attributed to *Neri di Bicci*.

fine courtyard, with porticoes, that contains Roman remains and various pieces of sculpture. The second courtyard, which was also very magnificent and where receptions and shows were held on the occasion of weddings and celebrations, has been rebuilt unsuccessfully. This palace used to contain many of the masterpieces that are now on view in the galleries and museums of Florence. Among the various rooms, important is the Chapel by Michelozzo, reached by going up the first staircase on the right in the courtyard. Here are the celebrated frescoes by Benozzo Gozzoli representing the *Journey of the Three Kings to Bethlehem* (1459-60) in which many personages of the time are portrayed: Lorenzo the Magnificent with his father, Piero the Gouty and his sisters, Galeazzo Maria Sforza, Sigismondo Malatesta, John VII Paleologus, Emperor of Constantinople, the painter himself and his master, Fra Angelico. There is also an interesting Gallery, reached by going up the second stairs, decorated with stuccoes and mirrors of the end of the 18th century, with a fine fresco by Luca Giordano on the vault, the *Apotheosis of the Medici dynasty* (1682-83).

The Basilica of San Lorenzo and the cupola of the Princes' Chapel. At the side: the facade of the basilica.

SAN LORENZO

An ancient basilica, consecrated in 393 by St. Ambrose, bishop of Milan, it was probably the first church to be built in the city and was then outside the city walls. Rebuilt in the 11th century, it was radically restored in the 15th century for the Medicis, for whom it was the family church. The interior, spacious, light and elegant, is one of the masterpieces of the early Florentine Renaissance; it is the work of Brunelleschi, who designed it in 1420 and directed the work from 1442 until his death in 1446. It is in the form of a Latin cross and has a nave and two aisles with side chapels. There are numerous masterpieces, including two bronze pulpits by Donatello at the end of the nave, the master's last work (about 1440), completed after his death by pupils; a fine marble tabernacle by Desiderio da Settignano (mid 16th century) opposite the pulpit on the right; the *Marriage of the Virgin*, a painting by Rosso Fiorentino (1523) in the second chapel on the right; a remarkable *Annunciation*, with *Scenes of the life of St. Nicholas of Bari* by Filippo Lippi (c. 1440) in the predella, in the left chapel of the left transept, where, opposite a nineteenth century monument to Donatello (who is buried in the vaults under the church) there is also a curious marble sarcophagus, attributed to Donatello, sculptured like a wicker basket; and also a large fresco representing the

Martyrdom of St. Laurence by Bronzino (1565-69) in the left aisle, opposite the pulpit. Finally, the Old Sacristy, exceptionally important, for its architecture and works of art, reached from the left transept. Elegant and of crystalline simplicity in its spatial conception, it fully expresses Brunelleschi's architectural idea (1420-29). Despite its small size it ranks as one of Brunelleschi's finest works. It is a chapel on a square plan, composed of a cube surmounted by a hemispherical cupola in sections outlined in pietra serena on white plaster, a decoration typical of Brunelleschi. The eight fine tondi in the lunettes and pendentives (4 with *Scenes from the life of St. John the Evangelist* and 4 with the *Evangelists*) are by Donatello, as are the two bronze doors beside the altar and a fine clay bust of *St. Laurence*; in the centre of the chapel, under a large marble slab, is the *tomb of Giovanni di Bicci dei Medici and of Piccarda Bueri*, the parents of Cosimo the Elder, by Andrea Cavalcanti (1434); on the left wall, under a large arch, is the *Tomb of Piero the Gouty and Giovanni dei Medici*, sons of Cosimo the Elder, by Andrea del Verrocchio, helped maybe by Leonardo.

At the side: **interior of the basilica.** Below: **bronze pulpit,** by *Donatello*.

LAURENTIAN LIBRARY

This library was founded by Cosimo the Elder and enlarged by Lorenzo the Magnificent; the entrance is in the beautiful cloister of San Lorenzo. It is extraordinarily rich in old manu-scripts and codices. Among the most important are the so-called Medici Virgil (4th-5th century), the Pandects of Justinian (6th century), the oldest existing examples of the tragedies of Aeschylus (11th century) and of the writings of Thucydides, Herodotus and Tacitus (10th century). Michelangelo began the building in 1524 and designed the entrance hall and the large, elegant reading room, while the vestibule was completed by Vasari and other architects.

At the side: *Brunelleschi's* **cloister in San Lorenzo.**
Below: **staircase** by *Michelangelo* **in the vestibule of the Laurentian Library.**

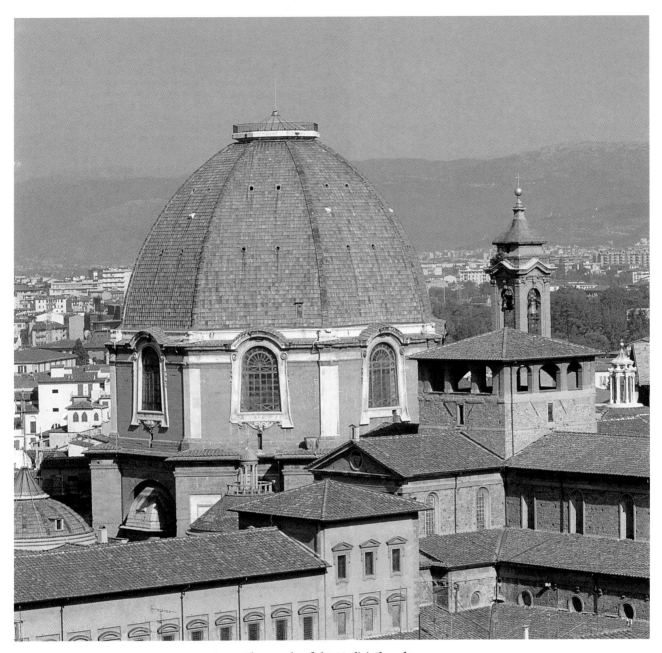

The cupola of the Medici Chapels.

MEDICI CHAPELS

The shrine and mausoleum of the Medicis, by the church of San Lorenzo (the entrance is at the back of the church in Piazza Madonna degli Aldobrandini), the Medici chapels are an important architectural and artistic complex, famous above all for the statues by Michelangelo. The Princes' Chapel is also impressive on the outside: its structure resembles that of the Cupola of the Cathedral, octagonal in form with small apses. Inside there is first a wide crypt, which leads to the sumptuous Princes' Chapel, ordered by Ferdinando I in 1602. Work began two years later from a plan by Matteo Nigetti, with the participation of Buontalenti, and continued for more than a century. The great octagon is entirely walled with inlays of hard precious stones and the effect is spectacular. Against the walls are the sarcophagi of six Medici Grand Dukes; above

those of Ferdinando I and Cosimo II, statues in gilt bronze by Ferdinando Tacca; below are sixteen coats of arms of Tuscan cities, also in inlaid hard stones; the high altar, in precious marble and hard stones, is a modern reconstruction, with pieces originating in various periods. The frontal has a representation of the *Supper at Emmaus*; the cupola is frescoed with *Scenes from the Old and New Testament*, by Pietro Benvenuti (1828). A corridor leads to the *New Sacristy*, the famous and beautiful chapel built by Michelangelo for Cardinal Giulio dei Medici, later Pope Clement VII. It was Michelangelo's first experience in architecture; he worked on it, through various vicissitudes, from 1520 until his patron, who had given him a completely free hand, died and he left Florence for good (1534). However the chapel was not finished. On a square plan,

The interior of the Princes' Chapel. Below: **two statues in gilded bronze,** by *Ferdinando Tacca.*

The interior of the cupola of the Princes' Chapel. Below: the coats of arms of Florence, Pisa and Siena.

Two works by *Michelangelo*. Left: **the Tomb of Giuliano, duke of Nemours.** Right: **the Tomb of Lorenzo, duke of Urbino.**

it resembles the structure of Brunelleschi's Old Sacristy, with ribbings in pietra serena on white plaster, but with much richer and more complex architectural decoration (niches, windows, arches etc.). Of the many tombs planned, the only ones completed were those of two minor members of the great Florentine family; Giuliano, Duke of Nemours, the third son of Lorenzo the Magnificent; an expert in political and military affairs, he was appointed by his brother, Pope Leo X, standard bearer of the papal army; he lived for a long time in France, where he received a dukedom from King Francis I, and died at the age of thirty-seven in 1516. The other is Lorenzo, Duke of Urbino, son of Piero the Unfortunate; like his father ill-suited to reign over a state, he received the dukedom of Urbino from his uncle Leo X but reigned for a very short time. He made a political marriage to a relation of the King of France, Madeleine de la Tour d'Auvergne, (1518); a brief union, because the wife died in childbirth in the following year, and Lorenzo, just twenty-seven, died six days later. Their daughter, Catherine, the last of the Medicis to descend from Cosimo the Elder, later became queen of France. The two twin tombs are seen against the splendid architecture: sculptured figures of the two men are placed over the sarcophagi, which are decorated with the famous allegorical statues. On the left, with his back to the altar, is *Giuliano* represented as an antique warrior in a cuirass, sublimely idealised; there is a story that when

people told Michelangelo that the statue did not look at all like the deceased, as appears evident from the paintings by Allori and Bronzino, he said that after ten centuries no-one would notice. On the sarcophagus are the figures of *Night*, reclining in sleep, and *Day*, muscular, vigorous, with strangely twisted limbs, the face unfinished. *Lorenzo*, on the right, is in a noble meditative posture (he is called "Il Pensieroso") with a warlike helmet on his head; at his feet, the melancholy dozing *Dusk* and the awakening *Dawn*, perhaps the most famous, the finest of all these statues. Over the sarcophagus containing the remains of Lorenzo the Magnificent and his brother Giuliano, killed in the Pazzi conspiracy, is the beautiful *Virgin and Child*, also by Michelangelo, at which the two dukes gaze; at the sides, *St. Cosma* (left) by Montorsoli and *St. Damian* (right) by Raffaello da Montelupo, works by two pupils of Michelangelo that fall far below the expressive achievement of the statues near them. This work by Michelangelo, though unfinished (the tomb of Lorenzo the Magnificent and Giuliano was finished off by Vasari) is generally interpreted as a lofty meditation on human destiny, its vanity and its redemption by religious faith. The three zones of the chapel can be understood in this sense: the lower order, with the tombs and allegorical statues, represents all-consuming Time that leads inexorably to death, to Hades; the middle band is the terrestrial sphere, and the upper one, more luminous,

LORENZO IL MAGNIFICO e GIVLIANO DEI MEDICI

Madonna and Child, by *Michelangelo* flanked by **Saint Cosma**, by *Montorsoli*, and **Saint Damian**, by *Raffaello da Montelupo*.

Right: **Madonna and Child,** by *Michelangelo*.
A masterpiece of sculpture, in which the wonderful twist of the body of Jesus becomes the moving, human gesture of a baby seeking its mother's breast; marvelous also the expression, sweet and sorrowful, of the Virgin as she gazes not at her Son, but beyond Him, towards His destiny.

with the lunettes and the cupola, the vault of Heaven: the sarcophagi are as it were interrupted in the middle by scrolls, thus liberating the souls of the deceased which go beyond every dimension in space and time, to their redemption by the eternal idea of Life (the Virgin and Child).

45

The statues of **Night** (above) **and Day** (below), **on the Tomb of Giuliano**, by *Michelangelo*.

The statues of Dusk (above) and Dawn (below), on the Tomb of Lorenzo, by *Michelangelo*.

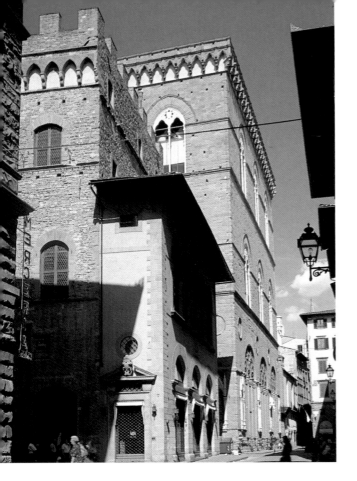

ORSANMICHELE

The religious and civic centres of Florence, Piazza del Duomo and Piazza della Signoria, are connected by Via Calzaioli, an elegant, busy shopping street, in which stands the square mass of Orsanmichele, a building erected for civic use and subsequently converted into a church. In 1284 the Florentine republic appointed Arnolfo to build a loggia for the collection and storage of grain, in the garden (orto) of the Monastery of San Michele — hence the name. This was burnt down in 1304, and rebuilt between 1337 and 1404 by Francesco Talenti and Neri di Fioravante in the elegant and ornate "decorated" Gothic style. The stores were kept on the two upper floors, the grain came down to the loggia below, through the supporting pillars and flowed out at the openings provided. The external decoration was contracted out to the various city Guilds; each had a tabernacle with its coat of arms and the statue of its patron saint. Remarkable, among the sculptures, are: the *Baptist* and *St. Matthew* by Ghiberti, *St. George* by Donatello (original in the Bargello) and the classical *Four Crowned Saints* by Nanni di Banco. The interior has a double nave with high cross vaults; in the right one, *tabernacle* by Andrea Orcagna (1359), a large Gothic cusped shrine, whose base is decorated with bas-reliefs of *Scenes of the life of the Virgin* and which contains the *Madonna of the Graces*, by Bernardo Daddi (1347).

The exterior and interior of Orsanmichele. Facing page: **the Tabernacle,** by *Orcagna*.

PIAZZA DELLA SIGNORIA

In Roman times, the area that is now the civic centre of the town was occupied by dwelling houses and the theatre. At the end of the 13th century the zone was included in the town-planning scheme directed by Arnolfo di Cambio, who requisitioned and pulled down the houses of Ghibelline families standing there and began to build Palazzo Vecchio. Henceforward the piazza became the setting for public speeches, ceremonies, meetings, uproars, executions: famous, especially, that of Gerolamo Savonarola, the preacher who was, for a short time, the arbiter of political life in the city, was excommunicated and burnt at the stake as a heretic on May 23rd, 1498, on the spot now indicated by a plaque. Now the piazza lacks unity owing to uncoordinated building around it, which went on until last century. The Gothic loggia was erected in the 14th century; a false Renaissance-style palace was built opposite Palazzo Vecchio in the nineteenth century. On the side opposite the Loggia, at N° 5, is the Alberto della Ragione collection (works of contemporary Italian art) and at N° 7, Palazzo Uguccioni, executed from a design by Michelangelo or Raphael, and on the other side the Tribunal of the Guilds, built in 1359.

Tribunale di Mercatanzia (Merchants' Court). Left: Equestrian monument to Cosimo I dei Medici, by *Giambologna*.

NEPTUNE FOUNTAIN

Bartolomeo Ammannati was employed by Grand Duke Cosimo I on the recommendation of Vasari. He worked as an architect on the rebuilding of the Pitti Palace, of the two bridges of Carraia and Santa Trinita, and on the building of many palaces in the city; as a sculptor, his most important work is this fountain in the piazza, commissioned by Cosimo and executed between 1563 and 1576. In the centre of the polygonal pool is the large figure of *Neptune* (a slight resemblance to Cosimo may indicate an intention to flatter him); beneath the statue is a coach drawn by sea-horses; all round and at the edge of the pool are the magnificent bronze figures of *Naiads*, *Tritons* and *Satyrs*, works that reveal the hand of Giambologna, who was Ammannati's assistant. The fountain has been damaged several times; one night during Carneval in 1830 a group of tipsy young men in masks bore off a Triton and threw it into the Arno; the statue was never recovered, and has been substituted by a copy. There are more statues on the steps of the Palace: the *Marzocco*, the lion symbolic of the Florentine republic, a copy of the original by Donatello (Bargello); a copy of Michelangelo's *David* (Gallery of the Accademia), brought here in 1504 to symbolise the liberty to which Florence aspired during the brief republican period; *Hercules and Cacus* by Bandinelli (1534) and two statuettes (perhaps Philemon and Baucis changed into plants) by De' Rossi and Bandinelli.

The Neptune Fountain, by *Bartolomeo Ammannati.*
Below: two details of the fountain.

Bird's eye view of the Loggia dei Lanzi.

LOGGIA DEI LANZI

This is also called the Loggia della Signoria because it was built to hold the public ceremonies of the Signoria under cover; or also the Loggia dell'Orcagna from the name of the architect who, according to Vasari, designed it. These Lanzi were the Lanzichenecchi (Landesknechts), German mercenaries in the pay of Cosimo I, who were housed in the building for a certain period. The Loggia was built between 1376 and 1383 by Benci di Cione and Simone Talenti. It consists of three large classical arches, on columns of different styles, leading to a large cross-vaulted porch. The lobed panels between the arches were executed between 1384 and 1389 from designs by Agnolo Gaddi and enclose statues of the *Virtues*. Piazza della Signoria became the scene of official functions and had to be a worthy setting for a state aspiring to be a Great Power; it was enriched with sculptures and the Loggia became a sort of open-air public museum. Two heraldic *lions* flank the entrance: the one on the right is of the classical epoch, the other is sixteenth century. Under the right arch is the *Rape of*

the Sabine Women, by Giambologna (1583); a work of refined virtuosity, which is a prelude to Baroque, it was principally conceived to present and solve technical and compositional problems, indeed the subject of the group was only decided at the last minute when the sculpture had been finished. The left arch frames the *Perseus* of Benvenuto Cellini (1546-54): the hero defeating the Medusa has the monumentality of Michelangelo together with the extenuated preciosity of contemporary Mannerism; the base is splendid, with statues and bas-reliefs that reveal the artist's skill as a goldsmith. Cellini was only able to complete the statue after solving many technical problems, and after ten years of entreaty to Cosimo to allow him the honour of sculpting something for Piazza Signoria. The loggia also contains *Hercules and Nessus*, another group by Giambologna, *Menelaus bearing the body of Patrocles*, a Roman copy of a Greek original of the 4th century B.C.; six Roman female statues and the *Rape of Polixena*, a fine work by the nineteenth century sculptor Pio Fedi.

The Perseus, by *Benvenuto Cellini.* Right: **The Rape of the Sabine Women,** by *Giambologna.*

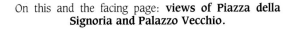
On this and the facing page: **views of Piazza della Signoria and Palazzo Vecchio**.

PALAZZO VECCHIO

Palazzo della Signoria, called Palazzo Vecchio, the old palace, after the middle of the 15th century when the Medicis left it and moved to Palazzo Pitti, was the residence of the highest authorities in the city, her political centre, (the Borough council is still housed there) and a symbol of the strength and harmony of established institutions. The building was begun in 1299 and was probably designed by the great architect Arnolfo di Cambio. The original edifice, a massive rusticated cube three storeys high, graced with fine two-lighted windows, is crowned by a gallery projecting on brackets, above which soars the beautiful and mighty tower; under the arches, between the brackets, are repeated the nine coats of arms of the Comune of Florence, including the best known, a red lily on a white ground. Some of the brackets have trap doors (machicolations) from which, in the not infrequent case of risings or revolts, stones, boiling oil and molten lead were thrown at assailants. The tower, 94 metres high, is, by a stroke of genius, placed off-centre, to echo the asymmetry of the piazza; it was finished in 1310. The palace was repeatedly enlarged, in 1343, in 1495 (by Cronaca) and in the 16th century by Vasari, who

Courtyard, by *Michelozzo.* Below: **the Hall of the Five Hundred.**

considerably altered the interior, by Giovanni Battista del Tasso and by Buontalenti. In 1323 a high balustrade was built on the two sides overlooking the piazza, from which the Republican authorities, the Priors and the Standard-bearer harangued the populace; this was removed in the last century. The interior of the palace is of the greatest interest both for the rooms themselves and the works of art. On the ground floor the fine courtyard by Michelozzo and the Arms Hall (entrance on the left side of the palace, opened only for temporary exhibitions); austere and bare, it is the only fourteenth century room that has been left unaltered, and is interesting on that account. On the first floor, the magnificent Hall of the Five Hundred, with the adjacent Study of Francesco I, the Hall of the Two Hundred by the brothers Da Maiano (1472-77) with a fine coffered ceiling in wood (this housed the Council of two hundred citizens who discussed wars and alliances, and is now used by the Borough Council); the apartments of Leo X, with a chapel and rooms frescoed with *Scenes of the Medici family* by Vasari and helpers (only the rooms of Leo X, Lorenzo the Magnificent and Cosimo I can be visited because the others are occupied by the Mayor and aldermen). On the second floor, the Apartment of the Elements, designed by Giovanni Battista del Tasso (c. 1550). These rooms too were decorated by Vasari and helpers, some with fine inlaid cabinets, and also the lovely Saturn Terrace with its splendid view; the Apart-

Hercules and Cacus, by *Vincenzo de' Rossi.* Below, left: **Hercules and Diomedes,** by *Vincenzo de' Rossi.* Right: **Victory,** by *Michelangelo.*

Victory over the Pisans at Torre San Vicenzo, a fresco by *Vasari.* Below: **the Hall of Leo X**
(Apartments of Leo X).

Study of Francesco I dei Medici.

View of Florence during the siege of 1530, by *Giorgio Vasari* (detail), in the Hall of Clement VII (Apartments of Leo X). At the side: **the Hall of Opi** (Apartment of the Elements).

ments of Eleonora di Toledo, wife of Cosimo I, where special mention should be made of the Gualdrada room, with another fine cabinet, in ebony and hard precious stones, and the chapel, entirely frescoed by Bronzino, who also painted the very fine altar-piece (*Pietà*, 1553);the chapel of the Signoria; the very fine Audience Hall, with coffered ceiling and marble doorway, both by Benedetto da Maiano, which contains a beautiful wooden bench designed by Vasari, the famous, dramatic bronze group by Donatello representing *Judith and Holofernes* (c. 1455) formerly on the steps in front of the palace; the magnificent and sumptuous Lily room with the Map room and the Chancery next to it; Machiavelli, of whom there is a coloured clay bust and a portrait here, worked in this room for several years as the Secretary of the Republic; and here is the original of the charming fountain in the courtyard, *Boy with a Dolphin*, by Verrocchio (1476). On the mezzanine (reached from the Apartment of the Elements) is a series of 15 rooms containing an important collection of works

Above, from the left: **the Room of Hercules** and **the Room of Caeres** (Apartment of the Elements). Right: **the Gualdrada Room** (Apartments of Eleonora).

of art recovered in Germany after World War II. Among the most remarkable things are the so- called *Lancellotti Discobolus*, the best Roman copy of the famous Miro Discobolus, (Greek, 5th century B.C.) which has disappeared, like almost all the Greek originals; the *Crouching Aphrodite*, Roman sculpture, 2nd century A.D.; two fine coloured panels in *opus séctile*, 331 A.D.; Greek and Roman reliefs and sculptures of various epochs. Of medieval and modern art: a beautiful little painting on wood of the *Madonna of Humility* attributed to Masolino and another very small one attributed to Masaccio; a large *Nativity* by Antoniazzo Romano; *Pygmalion and Galathea* by Bronzino; a fragment, barely rough-hewn but very fine, of the *Rondanini Pietà* by Michelangelo; *Venus and Mercury present their son Anteros to Jove*, by Paolo Veronese; *Leda and the Swan*, by Tintoretto; *Portrait of Elizabeth of Valois*, by Coelho; *Judith with the head of Holofernes* and a large *Equestrian portrait of Giovanni Carlo Doria* by Rubens; a beautiful *Portrait of an Unknown Man* by

The Lily Room (Apartment of the Priors). At the side: **Judith and Holofernes,** by *Donatello.*

Hans Memling; the *Ecstasy of St. Cecilia* by Bernardo Cavallino; an exquisite *Portrait of Felicita Sartori* by Rosalba Carriera; Venetian landscapes attributed to Francesco Guardi and the circle of Canaletto; and lastly the pathetic *Maternity* by the nineteenth century German painter Friedrich von Amerling. Also on the mezzanine are the Museum of Musical instruments, containing rare and antique instruments of various periods, and the Loeser Collection, an important legacy of sculptures and paintings by Tuscan artists from the 14th to the 16th century. The most important works are: in sculpture, two terracotta groups representing soldiers and knights, by Giovan Fracesco Rustici (16th century); a splendid *Madonna and Child*, in painted wood, attributed to the school of Arnolfo di Cambio and a marble *Angel* by Tino di Camaino; in painting: the *Passion of Christ*, a curious work by Piero di Cosimo, end of 15th century: "an abstract and original spirit", Vasari called him in his *Life*; a *Virgin and Child* by Pietro Lorenzetti (first half of 14th century) and the remarkable *Portrait of Laura Battiferri* (wife of the sculptor Ammannati) by Agnolo Bronzino.

The Gualdrada Room or **Map Room** (Apartment of the Priors). Below: **two maps,** by *Ignazio Danti* and *Stefano Bonsignori*.

Piazzale degli Uffizi at night.

UFFIZI GALLERY

The Uffizi is not only the oldest art gallery in the world; it is the most important in Italy and also one of the greatest in Europe and in the whole world, visited by more than a million people every year. The gallery owns about 4800 works, of which about 2000 are on view (1000 paintings, 300 sculptures, 46 tapestries, 14 pieces of furniture and pottery, besides 700 more paintings kept in the Vasari corridor); the rest is in storage or on loan to other museums. This enormous quantity of works includes countless masterpieces, some being among the highest achievements of West-

ern art. The building containing the Gallery is itself splendid; it was built for Cosimo I in the mid 16th century in the zone between Palazzo Vecchio and the Arno, to house the public offices (hence the name); the 11th century church of San Pietro Scheraggio, and the old Mint, where florins were coined, were partly incorporated. The planning was entrusted to Giorgio Vasari, a great and eclectic figure in art at the time, court painter and architect, writer on art (his *Lives of the most excellent architects, sculptors and painters* is the most important source for the study of the history of

The loggia of the Uffizi overlooking the Arno. Below: view of the first corridor.

Above: **Madonna in Majesty,**
by *Giotto*.

*A departure from the Byzantine
tradition, already noticeable in
Duccio's Madonna (photo next
to it), is clearly evident and
reveals the beginning of a new
spatial depth.*

Above, left: **Madonna in Majesty,** by *Duccio di Buoninsegna*.

*Painted in 1285 for the Compa-
gnia dei Laudesi, the panel is
also known as the "Rucellai
Madonna" since it was originally in the Rucellai chapel in Santa Maria Novella.*

At the side: **Annunciation,** by
Simone Martini (1333); **Saint
Ansano and Saint Giulitta**, at
the sides, are by *Lippo Memmi*.

*The work of the Sienese painter
Simone Martini is poles apart
from the solid realism of Giotto;
he is the initiator of the so-
called Flamboyant or International Gothic style.*

Right: **Adoration of the Magi,** by *Gentile da Fabriano* (1456). *Painted for the Strozzi Chapel in the church of Santa Trinita, it is an exceptional example of Flamboyant Gothic style.*

Below: **The Battle of San Romano,** by *Paolo Uccello* (1456). *This large panel has a surprisingly "modern" look thanks to the abstract unreality of the colour and the foreshortening. This Tuscan artist was one of the first to study perspective.*

Italian art) who built it between 1559 and the year of his death (and that of Cosimo), 1574; the building, highly original, is erected over two long porticoes joined by a third side that opens on to the Arno with a magnificent arch of great scenic effect. The outside of the Uffizi is inspired by the style of Michelangelo's vestibule for the Laurentian Library, also with ribbing in pietra serena on white plaster. Together with the marvellous Corridor, it is certainly Vasari's masterpiece in architecture. Work on the Uffizi was resumed in 1580, by order of Francesco I, and directed by Bernardo Buontalenti, who built the large Medici Theatre (dismantled in 1890) and the famous Tribune; at the same time the top storey of the loggia was rebuilt, the offices were transferred elsewhere and some of the rooms were used for collections of works of art, arms, and scientific curiosities; and so the Gallery was born. The first nucleus of works already included paintings by Botticelli, Lippi, Paolo Uccello; about 1600 Ferdinando I had all the works at the Villa Medici in Rome transferred to the Uffizi; in 1631 Ferdinando II contributed an important collection of paintings, (originally in Urbino, the inheritance of his wife Vittoria della Rovere) including works by Piero della Francesca, Titian and Raphael; at the end of the 17th century Cosimo III collected gems, medals and coins and brought the *Venus*, later known as the "Medici" Venus, and other important antique sculptures from Rome; Anna Maria Ludovica, Electress Palatine, the last heir to the Medicis, enlarged the collection with Flemish and German paintings and left it in tis entirety to the state of Tuscany in her will (1743). The Lorraines also helped to enlarge the gallery's

Top: **Presentation of Jesus in the Temple,** by *Ambrogio Lorenzetti* (1342).

This work is the central part of a triptych painted for the Cathedral of Siena and great care was taken with the perspective, with effects of depth never before achieved in the painting of the time.

Bottom: **Adoration of the Magi,** by *Domenico Ghirlandaio* (1487).

To be noted are the elegant drawing, the clarity of the spatial construction and the brilliant colours, typical of the works of this artist.

Facing page: **Madonna and Child with Two Angels,** by *Filippo Lippi* (1465 ca).

The softness of the colours and the quality of the light which ties the figures in the foreground to the airy landscape in the background are particularly striking in this painting, originally in the Medici villa of Poggio Imperiale.

Above: **Madonna and Child with Saint Anne,** by *Masolino* and *Masaccio* (1424).

The Virgin and the Child, which recall the monumentality of Giotto's figures, are attributed to Masaccio. The enveloping figure of Saint Anne on the other hand is attributed to his master, Masolino.

Above, left: **Crucifix with the Magdalen,** by *Luca Signorelli* (early 16th century).

This is one of the most representative works of this artist from Cortona, famous above all for the cycle of frescoes in the cathedral of Orvieto.

Left: **Hercules and the Hydra**, by *Antonio del Pollaiolo*.

The small panel dating to around 1460 displays the particular care with which the artist treated movement, the nude and anatomy.

Facing page: **Portrait of a Young Man with a Medal depicting Cosimo the Elder,** by *Sandro Botticelli*.

Some hold that the young man may be the portrait of the artist (1474 ca).

The Madonna of the Magnificat, by *Sandro Botticelli*
(1482).

*This is one of the master's masterpieces of sacred art.
The tondo takes its name from the first word that
appears on the page of the open book in which the Virgin
is writing.*

artistic patrimony and Pietro Leopoldo (2nd half of the
18th century) reorganised it, appointed a Director, and
rearranged everything. In the nineteenth century, owing to the pillage of the Napoleonic wars, which was
only restored in part, and above all to the creation of
new specialised museums (Archaelogical Museum, Bargello, Fra Angelico Museum, Science Museums, Silver
Museum etc.) many works were removed from the
Uffizi and it became what it is today. Extensive restoration of many of the works has been effected since the
second world war, and is still in progress.

Facing page: two works by *Sandro Botticelli*. Above:
Spring or Primavera. Below: **The Birth of Venus.**

*Spring was the first to be painted (ca 1482-83). The title
derives from Vasari's interpretation, but the painting
actually represents the realm of Venus, as described by
Poliziano. The goddess is in a garden with Mercury (left)
blowing away the clouds, three Graces dancing, Spring
scattering flowers, Flora pursued by Zephyr and, above,
Cupid shooting an arrow. The Birth of Venus dates to
around 1484-86 and was also inspired by the poetry of
Agnolo Poliziano: Venus rises from the waters of the sea
and is blown to shore by the winds; an Hour of Spring
waits to cover her with a flowery cloak.*

Above: **The Madonna of the Goldfinch,** by *Raphael* (1506).
Here the artist achieves a marvelous synthesis of Leonardesque elements (the attitude and face of the Virgin) with echoes of Michelangelo (the pyramidal composition).

Above, left: **Coronation of the Virgin,** by *Sandro Botticelli.*

At the side: **the central panel of the Portinari Triptych,** by *Hugo van der Goes,* with the **Adoration of the Shepherds** (1478).
The artist was one of the greatest representatives of the minute and crystalline naturalism peculiar to Flemish art, and this painting strongly influenced the Florentine artists of the second half of the 15th century.

Holy Family with the Infant Saint John, by *Miche-langelo* (1504).

The painting, known also as the **Doni Tondo** *after the name of the patron, was painted when the artist was not yet thirty, and reveals Michelangelo's predilection for sculpture, to which painting always had a secondary role. The nudes in the background, perhaps influenced by Signorelli, are painted in muted tones, as if they were simulating a monochrome bas-relief.*

Above: **Annunciation,** by *Leonardo da Vinci* (ca 1470).

This early work of the master was painted in the workshop of Andrea del Verrocchio and comes from the monastery of Monteoliveto near Florence.

At the side: **The Madonna of the Harpies,** by *Andrea del Sarto* (ca 1517).

Painted for the convent of San Francesco in Florence, the picture takes its name from the two harpies carved on the base on which the splendid figure of the Virgin rests.

Facing page, below: **Death of Adonis,** by *Sebastiano del Piombo* (ca 1512).

This work dates to the artist's Roman period, when he came into contact with the art of Raphael and Michelangelo. In this composition the warm full-bodied figures are set in a country landscape with a hazy image of Venice in the background.

Flora, by *Titian* (ca 1515).

An early work of the master, still influenced by Giorgione, but already a prelude to the exuberant forms and intense colour tones of his maturity.

Benedetto Portinari, by *Hans Memling* (1487).

The gentle thoughtful expression, the careful execution, the soft landscape make this portrait one of the best works by this Flemish artist.

Above: **Landscape study,** by *Leonardo da Vinci* (detail). Left: **Study for Pallas,** by *Sandro Botticelli.* Below: **Study of two heads,** by *Leonardo da Vinci.*

Facing page: **Study of a man's head,** by *Michelangelo.*

THE DRAWINGS AND PRINTS COLLECTION

This collection of drawings and prints, now one of the greatest in the world, was begun by Cardinal Leopoldo dei Medici in the 17th century; when he died (1675) the material was brought from Pitti Palace to the Uffizi and was rearranged by Filippo Baldinucci, a scholar commissioned to do this by Cosimo III; it already amounted to about 100 volumes. The collection was then increased by legacies and purchases, and today reaches the considerable figure of more than 50,000 drawings and 60,000 prints by all the major Italian and foreign artists (only a few of them modern); these include Paolo Uccello, Fra Angelico, Botticelli, Leonardo, Michelangelo, Raphael, Brueghel, Dürer, Lorrain and countless others. The rooms are on the first floor of the Uffizi in the place of the former Medici Theatre, built by Buontalenti in 1585 for court festivities, balls and plays, and are reached by going up the magnificent staircase designed by Vasari. The large theatre, the first of the modern epoch, occupied most of this wing of the building and saw the birth of Melodrama (early 17th century). Application must be made to visit the Drawing and Print rooms which are only accessible to students: the first room is used for temporary exhibitions.

VASARI CORRIDOR

Conceived as a passage by air from the Grand Ducal Palace, Pitti, to the seat of government (the Uffizi), and, along another short passage, to Palazzo Vecchio, this singular feat of architecture and town planning was executed in the short space of five months, in 1565, by Giorgio Vasari, commissioned by Cosimo I. The Vasari Corridor starts from the Uffizi on the third floor between Room XXV and Room XXXIV, runs along the Arno over an arcade, crosses the river over Ponte Vecchio, passes between houses and palaces on the other side of the river, along beside the façade of the church of Santa Felicita (the Grand Dukes attended religious services there, unseen in a private box); it continues along the side of Boboli Garden and, after a distance of nearly a kilometre, enters the Pitti Palace. It was damaged in World War II and only reopened in 1973; one has to book visits in groups. About seven hundred paintings are on view, including seventeenth and eighteenth century Italian works, portraits of the Medicis and the Lorraines, and above all the famous collection of self-portraits, the most complete in the world, extending from the fourteenth century to the present time, including nearly all the greater Italian artists and numerous foreign ones.

Self-portrait, by *Diego Velazquez.* Below, left to right: **Self-portrait,** by *Jacques Louis David;* **Self-portrait**, by *Eugene Delacroix.*

Self-portrait, by *Gian Lorenzo Bernini.*

Piazza della Repubblica. Below: **the Column in the Market with the statue of Plenty.**

PIAZZA DELLA REPUBBLICA

In Roman times the city Forum stood where this piazza is today; there was a Temple of Jove and a column at the crossing of the two principal streets, *cardo* and *decumanus*, (respectively, the axis, Via degli Speziali - Via Strozzi, and Via Calimala - Via Roma). The Old Market, with its hovels, towers, loggias, stores and shops, all clustering round a column — henceforward known as the Column in the Market — on which was a statue of Plenty, replaced several times, superseded the Forum in medieval times. In 1571 Cosimo I decided to allocate part of the large district that had formed there to the considerable Jewish community in Florence; this measure was followed by restrictive provisions. Successive Grand Dukes were on better terms with the community in the Ghetto and Cosimo III granted the Jews the same rights as other citizens. In the 19th century, after an epidemic of cholera, the Comune decided to "wipe out centuries of squalor", as the plaque over the archway reads, and pulled down both Ghetto and market. In place of these, the pompous architecture of the modern square.

STRAW MARKET

This is the name given to the picturesque, busy little market of articles of Florentine craftsmanship that takes place on the corner of Via Porta Rossa and Via Calimala, under the Loggia del Mercato Nuovo, by Giovan Battista del Tasso (1547-51). On a square plan, the loggia was ordered by Cosimo I for some of the most important corporations such as the bankers and the dealers in gold, wool and silk. Beside it is the entertaining Boar Fountain (Porcellino) by Pietro Tacca (1612).

At the side: **the Boar Fountain**, by *Pietro Tacca*. Below: **the Palace of the Guelph Party**.

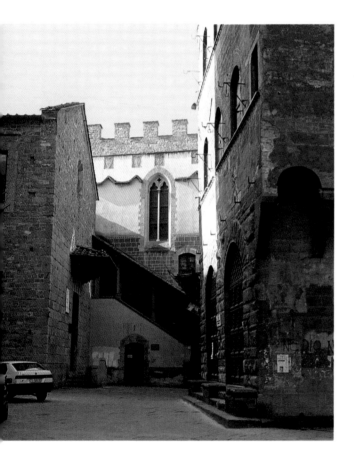

PALAZZO DI PARTE GUELFA

The Palace of the Guelph Party stands in the small piazza of the same name, one of the most picturesque places in medieval Florence. Built in the 14th century, it has a small, elegant façade with an outside staircase; it was enlarged in the 15th century (Brunelleschi took part in this work) and again by Vasari at the end of the 16th century. The powerful magistrature that it housed was established in 1267, when the Guelphs defeated the Ghibellines.

Palazzo dell'Arte della Lana (Woolmerchant's Guild).

PALAZZO DELL'ARTE DELLA LANA

The Woolmerchants' Guild, one of the most important in medieval Florence, built this palace to be its seat, joining together and rebuilding some previous constructions. As time passed the palace was rebuilt and transformed; in the 15th century it was connected with Orsanmichele by means of a fly-over bridge, by order of Cosimo I; in 1905 it was restored by Enrico Lusini and the fine frescoed rooms became the seat of the Dante Society. The 14th century Gothic Tabernacle of the *Madonna of the Trumpet* on the corner of Via dell'Arte della Lana and Via Orsanmichele has a *Madonna* by Jacopo del Casentino.

PALAZZO DAVANZATI

This stands in Via Porta Rossa, a narrow, picturesque street connecting Piazza Santa Trinita with Via del Calzaioli, at Piazza Davanzati. The palace, one of the finest and best preserved of the 14th century, was built for the Davizzi family and passed in 1578 to the rich, powerful Davanzati family, who added various parts to it, including the loggia at the end; it now houses the interesting Museo dell'Antica Casa Fiorentina (the old Florentine House Museum). Very picturesque is the porticoed courtyard, with a fine staircase leading up to the gallery round each storey. On the first floor is a hall with a fine cupboard for arms, and other furniture, a large table with an exquisite collection of caskets and some small 15th-16th century terracotta busts of the Florentine school; the delightful Parrot Room, whose walls are decorated with mock tapestry, with a fine 14th century fireplace; a small drawing room, with furniture and paintings of the 16th century; the beautiful Peacock Room, with decorated walls, a fine tabernacle (15th century) and a carved 16th century bedstead, which has a splendid and extremely rare white silk cover, embroidered with the *Story of Tristram* (14th century Sicilian

At the side: **Palazzo Davanzati, exterior.** Below: **cupboard,** by a *Sienese workshop* (early 16th century), intended for storing arms, as the inscription with the dedication to Mars indicates.

The Nuptial Chamber of the palace, with frescoes showing scenes from the story of the Chatelaine of Vergi (14th century). At the side: A Pope Saint, small polychrome wood statue, by *Pietro Alamanno*.

work); on the second floor, a hall like the first, with 16th century furniture; a room of early 16th century Florentine paintings; a study with other 14th - 15th century paintings and two painted chests; the magnificent Nuptial Chamber, with 14th century frescoes, two tabernacles and a chest full of contemporary linen. Lastly, on the third floor, the kitchen containing various utensils, crockery, a small loom and a curious chandelier with oil lamps. Many of the rooms have fine wooden ceilings, some of which are beautifully decorated, and dressers containing 14th - 17th century pottery; there are also some "place of ease", little rooms with the old latrines. Some of the rooms in the basement of the palace are used for temporary exhibitions.

Ponte Vecchio, seen from a terrace in Borgo San Jacopo. At the side: **Bust of Benvenuto Cellini,** by *Romanelli* (1900).

PONTE VECCHIO

As the name implies, (Old Bridge), the oldest bridge in Florence: it has, in fact, existed since the time of the Roman colony, when the piers were of stone and the roadway of wood; destroyed by flooding in 1117 it was completely rebuilt in stone but collapsed again in the terrible flood of November 4th 1333; it was rebuilt for the last time in 1345 (perhaps by the painter-architect Taddeo Gaddi) with three spans, very wide, planned with room for shops on either side. First of all the butchers settled there (but later also grocers, smiths, shoemakers etc.); these built the characteristic back shops projecting over the river, resting on supports and

A view of Ponte Vecchio with the shops of the goldsmiths. At the side: **the Mannelli Tower.**

Following pages: **Ponte Vecchio, the Arno and the hills,** seen from the windows of the second corridor of the Uffizi Gallery.

brackets. However, in 1591 Ferdinando I evicted them all to concede the shops to the goldsmiths only; and since then the bridge has been almost like a single shop window full of precious stones, interrupted only by two squares in the middle; the one looking downstream has a bust of Benvenuto Cellini, "master of the goldsmiths" by Raffaello Romanelli (1900). On November 4th 1966 the latest, dramatic flooding of Florence put the bridge to the test again: the structure itself stood up well, but the fury of the waters burst through the goldsmiths' shops at the back and swept away quantities of jewels.

SANTO STEFANO AL PONTE

St. Stephen at the Bridge stands in a small piazza on the left of Via Por Santa Maria; the first mention of the existence of a church here goes back to 1116; it was called *Sanctus Stephanus ad Portam Ferream*, St. Stephen at the Iron Gate, alluding to an old city gate near Ponte Vecchio. It has a simple Romanesque façade and a doorway decorated with marble in two colours (end of 13th century). The interior, with a single nave, was restored by Tacca in the 16th century; singular, and highly elegant, is the structure of the presbytery, preceded by a flight of steps by Buontalenti (1574) with a large altar on either side; there is a 16th century choir with a wooden ceiling: at the third altar on the left, bronze frontal with the *Martyrdom of St. Stephen*, by Tacca.

The church of Santo Stefano al Ponte.

SANTA FELICITA

This church stands in the small piazza of the same name, off the street leading from Ponte Vecchio to the Pitti Palace. It was erected on the site of an early Christian basilica of the 4th century; several times rebuilt, the last time by Ruggieri in the 17th century. The Vasari Corridor runs along the front part of the church, at the top; there is a box, opening in this, from which the Medici family and court took part in religious services, getting there directly from Pitti Palace without going out of doors. Inside, on the altar of the Capponi Chapel (first on the right) is a *Descent from the Cross*, by Pontormo (c. 1528); on the right wall an *Annunciation*, also by Pontormo; in the sacristy, a *polyptych* by Taddeo Gaddi.

The interior of Santa Felicita.

Pitti Palace. At the side: **the interior courtyard of the palace,** by *Bartolomeo Ammannati.*

PITTI PALACE

By the middle of the 15th century power was practically in the hands of the Medici family; Cosimo the Elder governed Florence from his new palace in Via Larga; Luca Pitti, at one time his friend, now led the faction that was most hostile to him and to his son Piero. Luca, belonging to a rich family of merchants, thought it was very important that he should own a palace finer than the one that Michelozzo was building for the Medicis. He chose the site, on the hill of Boboli, and commissioned Brunelleschi to design a building with windows as large as the doorways of the Medici palace and dimensions such that this would have fitted into his courtyard. Brunelleschi accepted with alacrity (his own plan for Via Larga had been rejected at the time) and produced the plans about 1445. Work began in 1457 (after the master's death) under the direction of Luca Fancelli, Brunelleschi's pupil. The façade overlooking the piazza consisted only of the seven central windows; it was of three storeys separated by slender balconies and covered with rusticated stone. At the death of Luca Pitti in 1473 the palace was still incomplete; then the Pitti family fell into disfavour, and, by the irony of fate, work on it was begun again by the Medicis themselves, that is by Eleonora di Toledo, the wife of Cosimo I, who bought the building and the land behind it in 1549. In the 16th and 17th century this became the palace of the Medicis, who enlarged it, created a garden on the Boboli hill, lengthened the building to nine windows each side, employing Giulio and Alfonso Parigi, and decorated the interior sumptuously. In the 18th century Ruggieri and Poccianti built the two-porticoed side wings that enclose the piazza. The remarkable fact is that each successive enlargement substantially respected the original design by Brunelleschi, both in form and material. During the period in which Florence was the capital of Italy (1865-71) the palace was the residence of Vittorio Emanuele II. Since 1919 it has been the property of the Italian State, together with its magnificent collections formed in centuries of devotion to art. There are seven museums here: the Palatine Gallery, the Royal Apartments, the Silver Museum, the Gallery of Modern Art, the Gallery of Costume, the Coach Museum and the Porcelain Museum.

Marble relief, showing a mule transporting the construction material for the palace. Below: **The Artichoke Fountain,** by *Francesco del Tadda,* in the Boboli Gardens.

The Madonna of the Chair, by *Raphael.*

PALATINE GALLERY

The Palatine Gallery has its own particular character: it is not an organic collection systematically arranged to present a "comprehensive review" of the art of a certain period or periods (like the Uffizi); it is, rather, a typical 17th century picture gallery that reflects the taste of its creator and hence of contemporary fashion; even the arrangement of the pictures manifests a decorative intention alien to the museographical criteria of today. This is, in fact, the charm of the Palatine Gallery, a "private" museum, almost a home, with its elegant furniture, ornaments, ebony cabinets, inlaid tables, stuccoes, tapestries and fine cornices. The idea of this collection goes back to two of the last Medicis, Cosimo II and Ferdinando II, who commissioned a great Baroque decorator, Pietro da Cortona, to fresco some of the rooms on the first floor of the Pitti Palace with allegorical mythological subjects celebrating the glories of the house of Medici (1641-47); he began to arrange pictures in these rooms, creating a new family collection to complement that already existing in the Uffizi. The Lorraines continued both with the decoration of the rooms and the collection of works of art; in 1828 Grand Duke Pietro Leopoldo opened the museum to the public, a liberal gesture quite in the spirit of the new European tendency towards a greater diffusion of culture. Limited at first to the fine rooms of Venus, Apollo, Mars, Jupiter and Saturn, the collection grew to its present dimensions until 1928, when a great number of paintings were exchanged with the Uffizi and many 16th and 17th century works were acquired.

Above: **Portrait of Agnolo Doni,** by *Raphael* (1505).

*This painting, which shows the
influence of Perugino, portrays
the man who commissioned the
Doni Tondo from Michelangelo.*

Above: left: **The Grand-ducal
Madonna,** by *Raphael* (1506).

*This painting was a great fa-
vourite with Ferdinand III,
hence the name.*

At the side: **Ezechiel's Vision,**
by *Raphael* (1518).

*This small panel is a late work
and belongs to the artist's Roman period, more clearly influenced by Michelangelo.*

Facing page: **The Veiled Woman,** by *Raphael* (1516).

*This marvelous portrait belongs
to the same Roman period as
the Madonna of the Chair. The
woman depicted has sometimes
been identified with the "Forna-
rina", the painter's beloved.*

Madonna in Glory and Four Saints, by *Andrea del Sarto.*

Above: **The Assumption of the Virgin with Apostles and Saints,** by *Andrea del Sarto* (1526).

Known also as the Panciatichi Altarpiece, after the man who commissioned it, it became part of the Medici collections in the 17th century.

At the side: **Holy Family,** by *Andrea del Sarto* (1529).

The picture was painted for Ottaviano dei Medici by the artist whom Vasari called "the painter without errors".

Previous page: **Events from the Life of Joseph Hebrew,** by *Andrea del Sarto* (1520-23).

The two panels once decorated the bedroom of Pier Francesco Borgherini, together with other panels by Bachiacca, Granacci and Pontormo (now in various European museums). Recent restoration has once more given the colours their original brilliance.

At the side: **Deposition,** by *Fra Bartolomeo* (1516).

This is the master's last work. The figures of Saints Peter and Paul in the background came to light during recent restoration, which also restored the vivacious colouring to the painting.

Below, left: **Portrait of a Lady,** by *Sandro Botticelli*.

The young woman in the picture has sometimes been identified as Simonetta Vespucci, Giuliano dei Medici's beloved. The painting has also been attributed to Ghirlandaio.

Below: **Madonna and Child with the Infant Saint John,** by *Sandro Botticelli*.

Above: **The Magdalen,** by *Titian* (1531).

Painted for the Duke of Urbino, this is one of Titian's most famous pictures. In the warm tones of the flesh, the brilliant auburn of the mass of hair, Titian's sense of colour here finds one of its finest expressions.

Above, right: **Saint Jerome,** attributed to *Piero del Pollaiolo.*

The attribution dates to an inventory of the Medici collections carried out in the 17th century, but the style of the painting is quite unlike Piero's traditional style.

At the side: **Concert,** by *Titian* (ca 1510).

Bought in 1654 by Leopoldo dei Medici as the work of Giorgione, it has only recently been given to Titian.

Portrait of a Gentleman in a Fur Coat, by *Paolo Veronese.*

A splendid portrait clearly influenced by Titian. For a long time the person portrayed was identified with the noble Venetian humanist Daniele Barbaro.

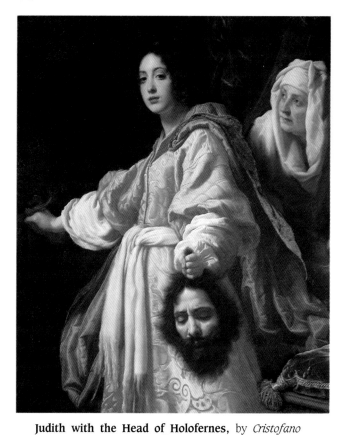

Judith with the Head of Holofernes, by *Cristofano Allori.*

Traditionally the horrid severed head of Holofernes is considered the self-portrait of the artist and Judith that of the woman whom the painter passionately loved.

At the side: **The Broken Bridge,** by *Salvator Rosa.*

An imaginative scene, even though the poetical and classic landscape anticipates the painting of European Romanticism.

At the side: **The Three Ages of Man**, *Venetian school* (16th century).

The painting has been attributed both to Giovanni Bellini and to Giorgione. The pictorial characteristics of the picture, the colours that blend and fuse, the interest in psychological introspection, would seem to indicate the latter. It is, in any case, a work that fully partakes of the 16th century, the great period of Venetian painting.

Below: **Still Life,** by *Bartolomeo Bimbi* (Monumental Apartments).

The Throne Room.

ROYAL APARTMENTS

This is the name given to a series of richly decorated rooms on the first floor, formerly the residence of the rulers of the houses of Medici, Lorraine and Savoy. As a matter of fact the only ones who lived there permanently were the Medicis, from Cosimo I to Gian Gastone (died 1737) who used to stay in bed the whole time, governing the state, eating, or receiving guests or mistresses. He was succeeded by his sister Anna Maria Ludovica, who left the Grand Duchy to the Lorraine family. The Lorraines preferred to live in the Villa of Poggio Imperiale, while the Savoy family had a liking

for the Villa della Petraia, at Castello. The most interesting rooms are: the Green Room with 18th century Gobelin tapestries and a large 17th century cabinet; the Throne Room; the Chapel; the Parrot Room, the first of those forming the Apartments of Queen Margherita; the Yellow Room; the Queen's boudoir with oriental style decorations; the Apartment of Umberto I with fine portraits and furnishings; the Bona Room with frescoes by Poccetti, and the neoclassical White Room, the large and luminous palace ballroom, where temporary exhibitions are now frequently held.

The Dining Room, decorated by *Terreni* and *Castagnoli.* Below: **the Green Room.**

On these two pages: Four examples of the art of the German goldsmiths from the jewellery collection of the Palatine Electress: **Rooster, Fisherman, Siren** and **Knife-grinder.**

SILVER MUSEUM

This was instituted in 1919 and arranged on the ground floor of Pitti Palace, in the rooms that were used as the summer apartments of the Grand Dukes. Among the most interesting of these, from the point of view of decoration, are the Room of Giovanni da San Giovanni and the three successive ones, frescoed by Colonna and Mitelli between 1638 and 1644. The collection includes goldsmiths' work, enamels, cameos, crystal and work in hard stones collected by the Medicis and the Lorraines. Among the most important pieces are: vases in hard stones belonging to the Magnificent; 17th century German ivories; vase in lapis lazuli by Buontalenti (1583): the jewels of the bishop-princes of Salzburg; drinking cup belonging to Diane de Poitiers (16th century); relief of *Cosimo II in prayer*, (17th century).

Above: **Portrait of Madame Trentanove,** by *Vittorio Corcos.* Above, left: **Portrait of the Daughter of Jack la Bolina,** by *Vittorio Corcos.* At the side: **The Dance,** by *Giovanni Bastianini.*

GALLERY OF MODERN ART

This contains a representative collection of 19th century painting, especially Tuscan. The first group of rooms is devoted to neo-classical and romantic works: a *Head of Calliope* by Canova; *Hercules at the crossroads* by Pompeo Batoni, the *Battle of Legnano* by Cassioli, works by Benvenuti, Dupré and Bezzuoli. In the second group are paintings of the second half of the century, with particular emphasis on the Macchiaioli, the most important current in Italian art at that time; the *Man caught by the stirrup,* the *Cavalry Charge* and the *Palmieri Rotunda* by Giovanni Fattori; works by Lega, Corcos and Signorini, and lastly paintings by Elisabeth Chaplin, Previati, Medardo Rosso and Vermehren.

The Amphitheatre. At the side: **The Bacchus Fountain**, by *Valerio Cioli.*

BOBOLI GARDEN

The creation of a garden on the hill at Boboli began at the same time as the rebuilding of the Pitti Palace for Cosimo I and Eleonora di Toledo at about the middle of the 16th century. Niccolò Pericoli, called 'Il Tribolo', architect and sculptor, had the job of laying out the large area to make it harmonize with the palace, according to the new Renaissance (and later Baroque) conception of the garden which, no longer a "private" *viridarium* or greenery, generally small, as was the custom in the Middle Ages, became, in the Renaissance, the symbol of a prince's power, the scene of parties and plays, a place of relaxation for the court, whre one could wander through groves full of allegory, populated with statues, grottoes, fountains. Boboli underwent many alterations owing to variations in taste, but the design remained substantially the same. Near the entrance is the curious Bacchus Fountain in which Valerio Cioli portrayed a dwarf of the court of Cosimo I astride a tortoise; further on is the Grotto by

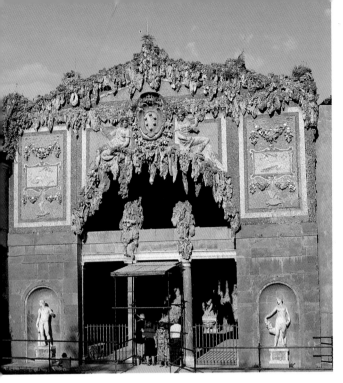

Buontalenti, built between 1583 and 1588 for the eccentric Francesco I; the first chamber is like a real cave in decoration with sculptured forms that, looked at closely, appear as animals; in the corners are four copies of Michelangelo's *Prisoners* (Accademia Gallery) which used to be here; in the cave behind, the group of *Paris and Helena*, by Vincenzo de' Rossi; last comes a small grotto with a *Venus* by Giambologna. Going on one comes to the Amphitheatre, first made in grass in the 16th century and remade in the 18th, for the performance of plays; the obelisk in the centre was brought to Rome from Luxor in the Imperial epoch. Going up to the left one comes to the Neptune fishpond and the Knight's Garden, where the Porcelain Museum is; or going straight on, along a wide avenue, one reaches the beautiful Island Square, with its large pool and island planted with lemon trees and the Ocean Fountain by Giambologna. The garden is full of other antique and Renaissance statues.

At the side: **The Buontalenti Grotto.** Below: **a view of the Boboli Gardens.**

The Ocean Fountain, by *Giambologna*. Below, left: the so-called "Viottolone". Right: the entrance to the Ocean Fountain.

The church of Santo Spirito on the square of the same name.

SANTO SPIRITO

The church of Santo Spirito stands on the south side of the Arno, in one of the working class districts of the city, and looks on to a simple piazza planted with trees, which is often enlivened by the stalls of a market. The original plan, made by Filippo Brunelleschi in 1444, was for a church facing in the opposite direction, with the façade towards the Arno overlooking a large piazza; but it could not be carried out owing to the opposition of the landowners involved. Brunelleschi's design was largely respected as regards the interior, executed after the master's death by Antonio Manetti and other pupils; while the simple façade is 17th century. The slender, elegant bell-tower was built by Baccio d'Agnolo at the beginning of the 16th century. The spacious and solemn interior recalls the symmetry and rhythmical perfection achieved by Brunelleschi in San Lorenzo, with the variation of a cupola over the presbytery and the continuation of the side aisles in transepts and an apse. The Baroque high altar, an elaborate work by Giovanni Caccini (1608) stands in the centre of the presbytery. In the right transept is a fine *Virgin and Child with Saints*

and the Commissioners by Filippo Lippi (c. 1490) with an interesting view of Florence in the background. In the apse is a polyptych by Maso di Banco representing the *Virgin and Child with Saints*; on a nearby altar is a painting of the *Holy Martyrs* by Alessandro Allori (1574); in the predella is a view of the first façade of Pitti Palace. In the left transept is the Corbinelli Chapel, an elegant piece of architecture and sculpture by Andrea Sansovino (1492); next to it is the *Holy Trinity with Sts. Catherine and Magdalen*, attributed to Francesco Granacci. Off the left aisle is an elegant vestibule by Cronaca (1494) with a fine barrel vault; this leads into the beautiful octagonal Sacristy, with cupola, by Giuliano da Sangallo (1492). Leaving the church, on the right is the entrance to the Cenacolo (Last Supper). This was in the refectory of the Augustinian monastery that used to stand here; the wall at the end of the room is covered by a large fresco by Andrea Orcagna (c. 1360) representing two scenes, one above the other: a wonderful *Crucifixion* and a *Last Supper* (now in a very poor condition).

At the side: **the nave.** Above: **Madonna Enthroned and Saints with Tanai de' Merli and his Wife,** by *Filippino Lippi* (1490). Below: **Trinity with Saint Catherine and the Magdalen,** attributed to *Francesco Granacci.*

The church of Santa Maria del Carmine. Facing page: the Brancacci Chapel.

SANTA MARIA DEL CARMINE

With Santo Spirito, this is the most important church on the south side of the Arno. It was founded in 1268 by the Carmelite Friars. In 1771 it was burnt down, except for the Corsini and Brancacci chapels and the sacristy; the parts destroyed were completely rebuilt a few years later. The unfinished façade is a high, severe wall of rough stone. The interior is prevalently 18th century; a 17th century masterpiece is the Corsini Chapel, at the end of the left transept, by Silvani and Foggini, with ceiling frescoed by Luca Giordano with the *Apotheosis of St. Andrea Corsini* (1682). At the end of the opposite transept is the main feature of the church: the Brancacci Chapel, whose frescoes mark a crucial moment in the history of Western art. The decoration of the chapel was begun in 1425 for Felice Brancacci, a rich Florentine merchant and diplomat. He commissioned Masolino da Panicale, a painter still sharing the Gothic taste but also open to the new ideas that were beginning to appear in Tuscan painting at the time; and the pioneer, the great master of this renewal was the colleague that Masolino chose to work with him on the Brancacci Chapel, Masaccio. The latter took the older painter's place perhaps in the following year, when Masolino was called to the court of Hungary, but for reasons unknown (perhaps his extreme poverty obliged him to leave the city), he did not finish the work, which was completed by Filippino Lippi between 1481 and 1485. Masaccio did the best work of his brief career (he died in 1428 at the age of 27) in the Brancacci Chapel: his frescoes won the unconditional admiration of Verrocchio, Fra Angelico, Leonardo, Botticelli, Perugino, Michelangelo and Raphael: his capacity to render the moment pregnant with the event, his historical sense of the Gospel words, his highly expressive dramatic gift, his natural style bare of all superfluous ornament, recall the impact of Giotto, but also make him the first great master of the Italian Renaissance. The cycles of illustrations on the walls of the Brancacci Chapel are two: *Original Sin* and *Scenes from the Life of St. Peter*; among the most significant are the *Expulsion from the Earthly Paradise*, a powerful masterpiece by Masaccio which faces the *Temptation of Adam and Eve*, by Masolino, on the wall opposite; *St Peter heals the lame man and restores Tabitha to life*, by both artists; *St Peter baptises the neophytes*, by Masaccio; *the Payment of the Tribute money*, and *St Peter heals the Sick*, also by Masaccio.

A few pictures of the frescoes in the Brancacci Chapel, by *Masolino* and *Masaccio.*

Facing page, from top to bottom and left to right: **Payment of the Tribute,** by *Masaccio*; **Temptation of Adam and Eve,** by *Masolino*; **Expulsion from the Earthly Paradise,** by *Masaccio.*

PIAZZA DI CESTELLO

This quiet piazza overlooks the Arno in the working-class district of San Frediano, among austere late 17th century buildings; on its left the Seminario Maggiore, in which there are fine illuminated manuscripts and books of anthems of the 11th-14th century; on the right, a barracks, once the granary of Cosimo III; opposite, with a rough, unfinished façade, is the church of San Frediano in Cestello (1680-89), designed by Antonio Ferri, as was the elegant cupola (1698); the fine Baroque interior alsocontains the exquisite *Smiling Madonna*, a coloured wooden statue of the Pisan school, 13th century. Not far from the piazza is the impressive city gate of San Frediano, 1332-34, perhaps by Andrea Pisano; this still has the original massive wooden door panels.

The church of **San Frediano in Cestello.** Below: **Santa Trinita Bridge.**

SANTA TRINITA BRIDGE

After Ponte Vecchio, this is certainly the finest and noblest in the city. Built in 1252 and rebuilt several times, it now has the form given it by Bartolomeo Ammannati in 1567-70; at the ends are four statues of the *Seasons*, 1608. The best of these is the one representing *Spring*, by Pietro Francavilla (at the corner with Lungarno Acciaioli).

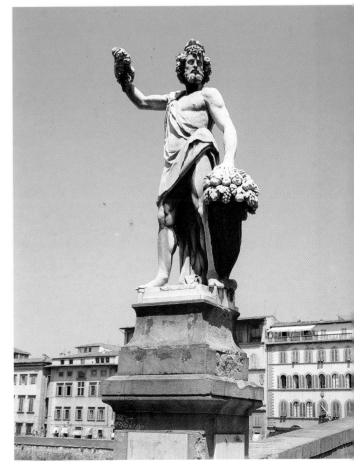

Above: **the interior of the Santa Trinita Bridge.** At the side: **Autumn,** one of the four statues which stand at the ends of the bridge.

PIAZZA SANTA TRINITA

Surrounded by noble mansions, the piazza is at the beginning of Via Tornabuoni, with the Column of Justice in the centre. This came from the Baths of Caracalla in Rome and supports the statue of Justice by Francesco del Tadda (1581). The fine large battlemented palace that extends as far as Lungarno Acciaioli is the 13th century Palazzo Spini-Ferroni (restored in the 19th century); at No. 1 of the piazza is the very fine Palazzo Bartolini-Salimbeni, the masterpiece of Baccio d'Agnolo (1517-20) with pleasant cross-shaped windows; the inscription on the lintel of the doorway (*carpere promptius quam imitari* – criticising is easier than imitating) – was put there by Baccio in answer to criticisms levied against the novelty of the architecture. The church of Santa Trinita goes back to the 11th century; the Mannerist façade is by Buontalenti (1593-94); the interior is very rich in works of art, that include: a wonderfully frescoed chapel (fourth on the right) with a painting on wood by Lorenzo Monaco (1420-25), a *Magdalen* in wood by Desiderio da Settignano (1464; fifth chapel on the left); the famous Sassetti Chapel (right transept); the tomb of Benozzo Federighi, a masterpiece by Luca della Robbia (c. 1450, left transept), and in the sacristy, the Renaissance tomb of Onofrio Strozzi, by Piero di Niccolò Lamberti (1421).

Spini-Ferroni Palace. Below: **the church of Santa Trinita.**

Three works by *Domenico Ghirlandaio* in the Sassetti Chapel in the church of Santa Trinita. At the side: **Adoration of the Shepherds**. Below, from the left: **Nera Corsi** and her husband **Francesco Sassetti**.

PIAZZA DEGLI ANTINORI

Via Tornabuoni leads from the Santa Trinita Bridge through Piazza Santa Trinita and ends in Piazza degli Antinori. The Antinori palace looking on to it was built between 1461 and 1466 perhaps by Giuliano da Maiano; the façade has three storeys in smooth rustication, with a projecting gutter above; there is a fine internal courtyard with a façade attributed to Baccio d'Agnolo (early 16th century). Opposite is the church of San Gaetano of antique origin (perhaps 10th century), once dedicated to St. Michael. In 1604 it passed to the order of Theatine friars and was rebuilt with large sums of money provided by Carlo dei Medici, (a cardinal, son of Grand Duke Ferdinando I) who wanted to atone for his sins. Work was begun by Matteo Nigetti and finished by Pier Francesco and Gherardo Silvani, who built the splendid Baroque façade (1648) with tall grooved pilaster strips and lively sculptured decoration. The interior is Baroque, sober and elegant; there is a singular Crucifix and Saints, by Filippo Lippi (Antinori Chapel) and the *Martyrdom of St. Laurence* by Pietro da Cortona (1635), one of the master's most important works.

Above: **Antinori Palace**. Below: **Strozzi Palace**.

STROZZI PALACE

Filippo Strozzi, a Florentine merchant of long-standing wealth (he had the merit of introducing into Tuscany not only the cultivation of artichokes, but also a good variety of fig), commissioned Benedetto da Maiano to build the palace in 1489; Benedetto was succeeded by Cronaca who directed the work until 1504. Later the construction was interrupted and resumed several times; the Strozzi family fell into disfavour in 1538, the palace was confiscated by Cosimo I dei Medici and given back 30 years later. Now it houses the Gabinetto Vieusseux and other cultural organisations; exhibitions are held here periodically, and the biennial Antiques Exhibition Fair. The massive building has a stone plinth all round it at the base, projecting like a bench; the exterior recalls that of Palazzo Medici-Riccardi, with pronounced rustication; at the top is a magnificent cornice by Cronaca; the two upper storeys have fine two-lighted windows; there is a majestic courtyard inside, also by Cronaca.

SANTI APOSTOLI

Going along Borgo Santi Apostoli from Piazza Santa Trinita one soon comes to a small piazza on the right, Piazza del Limbo, so called because there was probably a burial-ground here for children who died before they were christened. In this piazza is the Church of the Holy Apostles, erected in the 11th century and rebuilt in the 16th. It still has its fine stone Romanesque façade with a Latin inscription (apocryphal) attributing the foundation of the church to Charlemagne. The interior has a nave and two side aisles, and a fine trussed ceiling; in the third chapel on the right is an *Immaculate Conception* by Vasari; on the high altar a fine 14th century polyptych; in the left aisle a large glazed terracotta tabernacle by Giovanni della Robbia and the tomb of Oddo Altoviti, by Benedetto da Rovezzano.

Above: **the interior of the church of the Holy Apostles**; below: **Rucellai Palace.**

PALAZZO RUCELLAI

The wealthy merchant Giovanni Rucellai had several houses built along Via della Vigna Nuova, where he owned the whole district; these houses included the family palace (1446-51). The architect was Bernardo Rossellino, but he used a plan by the great Leon Battista Alberti. The palace shows the revival of classical form in harmony with the Florentine style. Alberti, one of the first architects to study ancient architecture, revives the use of three superimposed styles, with graceful pilaster strips, Doric, Ionic and Corinthian, supporting the trabeation; the result is of great elegance, which is also achieved in the fine courtyard. Opposite the palace is the charming Rucellai Loggia (1460-66), also designed by Alberti.

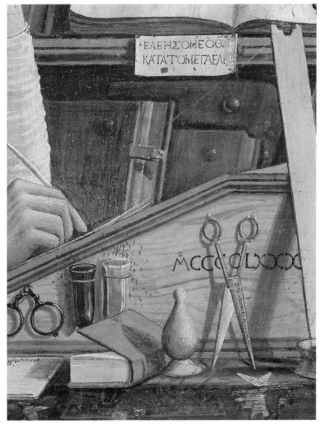

Saint Augustine in his Study, by *Sandro Botticelli* (1480). Right, above: **Saint Jerome in his Study,** by *Domenico Ghirlandaio* (1480); below: **detail.** Preceding page: **the church of Ognissanti.**

OGNISSANTI

The 13th century church of Ognissanti (All Saints) stands in the piazza of the same name overlooking the Arno. It was completely remade in the 17th century. The pleasing Baroque façade is by Matteo Nigetti (1637); the bell-tower is older (14th century). Inside are several paintings on wood and frescoes of the 15th-16th century, including the *Madonna of Mercy*, by Ghirlandaio, commissioned by the Vespucci family (the future great navigator Amerigo also appears in it; 1472). Beside the church is the refectory, with the famous *Last Supper* by Ghirlandaio; there are also two detached frescoes, formerly in the church: *St. Jerome in his study*, also by Ghirlandaio, and *St. Augustine in his study* by Botticelli.

The church of Santa Maria Novella on the square of the same name. Below: the interior.

SANTA MARIA NOVELLA

This great Dominican church stands on the site of a 10th century country oratory. It was begun in 1246; the first architects were Fra Sisto and Fra Ristoro. The size of this new church testifies to the importance of the religious orders in Florence at that time, also owing to their vital role as educators: Santa Maria Novella was the seat of the first public school in the city. The façade was begun in 1300, and the lower part was finished before the middle of the century, in the typical Florentine Romanesque - Gothic style. After the middle of the 15th century, Leon Battista Alberti, the great theorist of architecture in the Quattrocento, completed the inlaid marble façade by adding the central doorway and the upper part, of extraordinary elegance, with round window, tympanum and side scrolls. On the right side of the church is a garden, the old Plaona Cemetery, surrounded by sepulchres under Gothic arches. The interior shows the influence of Cistercian Gothic in the "softened" form that this style took in Italy; it is in the form of a Latin cross, with nave and side aisles and composite columns; an incredible number of works of art decorate the walls and chapels. In the second bay of the right aisle is the tomb of the Blessed Villana, by Bernardo Rossellino (1451); from the last bay one enters the 15th century Pura chapel and from this, the picturesque Cemetery. The right transept leads to the Rucellai Chapel; on the altar is a *Madonna* by Nino Pisano, in

Episodes from the life of the Virgin, frescoed by *Ghirlandaio* in the Sanctuary (details).

NATIVITAS TVA DEI GENITRIX VIRGO GAVDIVM ANNVNTIAVIT VNIVERSO MVNI the floor the tombstone of Leonardo Dati, by Ghiberti (1425). The chapel of Filippo Strozzi on the right of the high altar is entirely covered with frescoes by Filippo Lippi (c. 1500) with *Stories of Sts. Philip and John*; the tomb of Filippo Strozzi is by Benedetto da Maiano. The chapel of the main altar has frescoes by Domenico Ghirlandaio (c. 1495; the young Michelangelo was probably one of his assistants) with beautiful *Scenes of the Life of the Virgin*. The Gondi Chapel (on the left of the main chapel) has the celebrated *Crucifix* by Brunelleschi, the only sculpture in wood by the master to have remained to us. In the Strozzi Chapel (left transept) are frescoes by Nardo di Cione (c. 1367: remarkable representation of *Hell*). In the Sacristy nearby is a Crucifix, a youthful work by Giotto. Lastly, at the third bay of the left aisle, the marvellous *Trinity* by Masaccio (c. 1427) and the pulpit designed by Brunelleschi. Going out of the church, on the right, is the interesting group of Cloisters. The 14th century Green Cloister has frescoes in the lunettes by 15th century painters including Paolo Uccello, who executed the *Scenes from Genesis* (very fine is the *Flood*, c. 1430); on one side of the cloister is the entrance to the Spaniards' Chapel, a 14th century chapel frescoed all over, which, in the 16th century, was allocated to the Spaniards at the court of Eleonora di Toledo, the wife of Cosimo I. In the small Cloister of the Dead nearby is a 14th century stained glass window representing the *Coronation of the Virgin*, which used to be in the round window in the façade of the church.

On these two pages: **various frescoes in the Spanish Chapel,** by *Andrea di Bonaiuto.* Above: **the Church Militant** (detail); at the side: **the Triumph of Saint Thomas Aquinas, with the Virtues, the Sciences, the Doctors of the Church and the Defeated Heretics.**

Preceding page, above: **Descent into Limbo.** Below: **Resurrection** (detail).

The **"Tribune"** by *Emilio de' Fabris* (1882).

GALLERY OF THE ACCADEMIA

This is one of the most famous galleries in Italy, visited by thousands of people, especially owing to the presence of the *David* and of other famous sculptures by Michelangelo. The Gallery, (Via Ricasoli 60, near Piazza San Marco) was founded in 1784 by Grand Duke Pietro Leopoldo of Lorraine; at the same time the Academy of Fine Arts was instituted, to unite all the schools of art, drawing and sculpture already existing in the city; so the gallery was created with the specific purpose of helping the pupils to know and to study the Old Masters. Many of the works, however, came from a previous collection, that belonged to the Academy of the Art of Drawing, an institution of great prestige, founded in 1562 by Cosimo I. This included all the greatest artists of the time, and was based on the example of the 14th century Company of Painters of St. Luke. The collection of paintings, already considerable, was increased as a result of the suppression of churches and monasteries (1786 and 1808); there were further acquisitions and in 1873 the *David* was brought here,

Facing page: **the Four Prisoners,** by *Michelangelo*. Above, left to right: **the Prisoner known as Atlas, the Young Prisoner, the Prisoner Awakening** and **the Bearded Prisoner** (the first at the bottom left).

These imposing figures were part of the projected tomb of Pope Julius II, which was to have stood in the basilica of St. Peter in Rome (only partially realized).

Below, centre: **Saint Matthew,** by *Michelangelo*.

Perhaps sculptured in 1504, it is one of the earliest examples of Michelangelo's so-called "non-finito" or unfinished style.

Below, right: **Palestrina Pietà**, by *Michelangelo*.

This is one of the master's last works. Despite the high quality of the dramatic sculpture, some scholars refuse to attribute it to Michelangelo because there is no mention of it in historical sources.

followed in 1911 by the *Prisoners* and *St. Matthew*, while the *Pietà* only arrived in 1939, after its recovery from the antiques market. The Gallery also exhibits plaster models by Giambologna. There is a notable collection of paintings from the 13th till the early 16th century; among the most important works are: a *Crucifix*, Sienese school, second half of the 13th century (attributed by some people to the great Duccio di Buoninsegna); the *Tree of the Cross*, by Pacino di Buonaguida (early 14th century); a polyptych by Andrea Orcagna (mid 14th century) and works by his brothers, including a triptych by Nardo di Cione (1365) and a *Coronation of the Virgin* by Jacopo di Cione; 24 panels by Taddeo Gaddi (14 with *Scenes of the Life of Christ* and 10 with *Scenes of the life of St. Francis*; the very fine *Pietà* by Giovanni da Milano (1365); the *Adimari Chest*; a *Visitation* attributed to Domenico Ghirlandaio; the *Madonna of the Sea* and the youthful *Madonna and Child, little St. John and two Angels*, by Sandro Botticelli; *Trinity and Saints*, by Alesso Baldovinetti (1471).

On this page and the facing page: **David,** by *Michelangelo (1501-1504).*

The grandiose character of the work (the statue alone, without the base, is over 13 feet high), its dramatic tension, the proud, beautiful face, confidently gazing at the adversary, the precision of the anatomy and the muscles ready to spring, the superb moral and human dignity of the personality, all express the youthful vision of Michelangelo, who surrounds the Biblical champion with an atmosphere of heroism.

Above: **Enthroned Virgin,** by
Fra' Bartolomeo. Right, above:
**Madonna and Child, the In-
fant Saint John and Two Angels,** by *Sandro Botticelli.* At
the side: **Madonna and Child
with Saints,** another work by
Botticelli.

Preceding page, above: **Gallery
of the Accademia, room with
the Rape of the Sabine Wom-
en,** by *Giambologna.* Below,
left to right: **Assumption of
the Virgin and Saints,** by *Perugino;* **Annunciation,** by *Ma-
riotto Albertinelli.*

The church of San Marco.

SAN MARCO

Piazza San Marco has a prevalently modern look; the only medieval note is the 14th century loggia of the Accademia, once part of the former Hospital of St. Matthew, and now the entrance portico of the Academy of Fine Arts. On the corner with Via degli Arazzieri is the Palace of Livia (1775), built by Grand Duke Pietro Leopoldo for a circus dancer, Livia Malfatti. In the centre of the piazza are shrubs and trees and a monument to General Manfredo Fanti, by Pio Fedi (1873). One side of the piazza is occupied by the church and monastery of San Marco. There was a monastery of Silvestrini monks here from 1299 onwards; in the first half of the 15th century Cosimo the Elder assigned both the church and the monastery to the reformed Dominican monks of the Blessed Giovanni Dominici; this was partly by the desire of Pope Eugene IV, and partly in expiation of Cosimo's own misdeeds. He commissioned Michelozzo to carry out the work of restoration, and invested no less than 40,000 florins in it. In the following centuries there were several alterations, particularly to the church, which has now a late 18th century façade in a neo-cinquecento style. The interior was re-structured by Giambologna in 1588 and by Silvani in 1678; on the interior façade is a *Crucifix* by followers of Giotto; at the third altar on the right, a *Virgin in prayer* (Mosaic).

The interior of the church of San Marco. Below: the Cloister of Saint Antoninus, by *Michelozzo.*

Enthroned Madonna and Child with Saints, by *Fra Angelico.* Facing page: **Saint Domenic at the Foot of the Crucifix,** by *Fra Angelico.*

MUSEUM OF SAN MARCO

The entrance to the monastery of San Marco is beside the church. This was one of the most important centres in Florence in the 15th century, thanks to the favour it held with Cosimo the Elder and Lorenzo the Magnificent, the unquestioned authority of its prior, St. Antonino, and the fact that it housed Savonarola, Fra Angelico and Fra Bartolomeo. Fra Angelico was one of the greatest artists of the 15th century; he infused the new, robust form inherited from Masaccio with a spirit that was still Gothic, to express a mystical, contemplative religious experience. The Cloister of St. Antonino, by Michelozzo, has frescoed lunettes and there are

some interesting rooms opening on to it; The Pilgrims' Hospice contains an exceptional series of paintings on wood by Fra Angelico: the *Flax-growers' tabernacle,* the *altar-piece from the convent of Bosco ai Frati,* the *Annalena altar-piece,* the *Descent from the Cross,* the *Last Judgement.* The Chapter-house contains a magnificent *Crucifixion* by Fra Angelico. The artist also decorated the Dormitory on the first floor; the series of cells has such masterpieces as the *Annunciation, Noli me tangere,* the *Transfiguration* and the *Coronation of the Virgin.* In the Prior's Apartment is a *Portrait of Savonarola,* who lived in these rooms, by Fra Bartolomeo.

VIRGINIS INTACTE CVM VENERIS ANTE FIGVRAM PRETEREVNDO CAVE NE SILEATVR AVE

Above: **Annunciation,** by *Fra Angelico.*

This is one of the artist's most famous compositions. A delicate and harmonious scene, set in a Michelozzian portico, surrounded by a garden.

At the side: **Flight into Egypt,** panel of the door of the Silver Cupboard, by *Fra Angelico.*

This is one of the most famous scenes of the thirty-five remaining panels of the forty-one originally on the Silver cupboard, where the most precious reliquaries and ex-votos of the church of Santissima Annunziata were kept.

138

At the side: **Deposition**, by *Fra Angelico* (1433-40).

Originally in the sacristy of Santa Trinita, and also known as the Santa Trinita Altarpiece, this Deposition is one of the culminating moments in Fra Angelico's painting.

Below, left: **Noli me tangere**, by *Fra Angelico*.

The painting depicts the meeting of the Magdalen and the Risen Christ in a charming, almost unreal, setting of a flower garden.

Below, right: **Crucifixion with the Virgin, Saint Domenic and Angels**, by *a collaborator of Fra Angelico.*

Above: **Virgin and Child Enthroned with Saints,** by *Fra Angelico* (1450 ca).

This composition is also known as the "Madonna of the Shadows" because of the shadows cast by the architecture on the right of the observer by the light which arrives from the window which actually illuminates the corridor in which the painting is to be found.

At the side: **The Sermon on the Mount,** by *Fra Angelico* and *collaborators.*

The design of the scene with its circular motif, often to be found in the works of the master, is undeniably by Fra Angelico.

Above: **Crucifixion,** by *Fra Angelico* (1442).

On the whole by the master's hand, the touch of Fra Angelico's collaborators is to be found only in the busts of the Dominican saints, depicted in the medallions, and in the busts of the prophets.

At the side: **Imposition of the Name on the Baptist,** by *Fra Angelico* (1435).

This may be a predella panel of the Annunciation now in the Museum of the Prado.

PIAZZA DELLA SANTISSIMA ANNUNZIATA

This elegant, regular square is surrounded on three sides by porticoes; on the right, the Hospital of the Holy Innocents; opposite, the church of the Santissima Annunziata, on the left, the Palace of the Servants of Mary, erected in imitation of the Hospital of the Innocents by Antonio da Sangallo and Baccio d'Agnolo. The building on the corner of Via dei Servi on the left is Palazzo Grifoni, by Ammannati (1563). In the centre is the statue of *Grand Duke Ferdinando I* begun by Giambologna and finished by Tacca (1608).

At the side: **one of the fountains which ornaments Piazza della Santissima Annunziata,** the work of *Pietro Tacca* (1629). Below: **the church of the Santissima Annunziata and the Monument to Grand-duke Ferdinand I.**

Cloister of Vows in the church of the Santissima Annunziata. At the side: small marble temple, by *Michelozzo,* which houses the Annunciation, of *Florentine school* (14th cent.).

SANTISSIMA ANNUNZIATA

In 1250 seven young Florentines, later beatified as the Seven Saints, founded the order of the Servites, or Servants of Mary, and began to build a shrine dedicated to the Virgin. The church was rebuilt by Michelozzo in the 15th century, and later by Antonio Manetti who, with the collaboration of Leon Battista Alberti, concluded the design of the circular Tribune at the end of the single nave. The porch on the piazza is late 16th century. Between this and the church is the Cloister of Vows, decorated with fine early 16th century frescoes by Andrea del Sarto, Pontormo, Rosselli, Franciabigio and other Mannerists. Inside the church, which was restored and embellished in the Baroque period, is a small 15th century Temple, immediately on the left on entering, that contains a greatly venerated 14th century Florentine school *Annunciation,* which legend attributed to the hand of an angel. Among the many works of art, mention should be made of two lecterns in the form of eagles (15th century English work) in the elegant Tribune; *Jesus and St. Julian* by Andrea del Castagno (c. 1455, first altar on the left) and the *Trinity* by the same (second altar on the left). Beside the church are the buildings of the Monastery which include the Cloister of the Dead.

The Hospital of the Holy Innocents. Below: the Cloister of the Hospital of the Holy Innocents, by *Filippo Brunelleschi*.

HOSPITAL OF THE HOLY INNOCENTS

In 1419 the Guild of Silk Merchants decided to purchase a piece of land and build a hospital to receive the foundlings or "Innocents", that is, children who had been abandoned. Brunelleschi was commissioned to provide the plan, by which he determined the architecture of the whole piazza on which the hospital faces, creating a portico whose proportions required the uniformity of all the buildings erected there. We can see here how the Renaissance conception of "planning" was replacing the casual building that went on in the Middle Ages, when one building was put up beside another in a completely different style. The hospital was finished in 1457; the front consists of nine wide arches on columns that stand at the top of a flight of steps; above these, a low upper storey which has windows with a tympanum; between the arches, glazed terracotta tondi by Andrea della Robbia. Inside are the cloisters by Brunelleschi and a gallery of works mostly of the 15th century. The collection includes: an *Annunciation* by Giovanni del Biondo; *Adoration of the Magi* by Ghirlandaio; a *Madonna and Child with Angels* by the school of Perugino; the *Madonna of the Innocents*, attributed to Pontormo and a *St. Sebastian* by Andrea del Sarto.

ARCHAEOLOGICAL MUSEUM

Cosimo the Elder was a keen collector of coins, goldsmiths' work and antique sculptures, a passion shared by the later Medicis. The Lorraine family began the collection of Egyptian antiquities, and encouraged independent excavation; in 1828 Leopoldo II subsidized an archaeological expedition in Egypt and Nubia led by the famous Champollion and the Italian Rossellini. In 1880 the collection was housed in its present seat, Palazzo della Crocetta in Via della Colonna, built by Giulio Parigi in 1620. The museum is divided into three sections: the Etrurian Topographical Museum, the Etrusco-Graeco-Roman Antiquities, and the Egyptian Collection. On the ground floor are two rooms arranged didactically: the famous *François vase* and the *Mater Matuta* are kept here. The pleasant garden contains reconstructions, partly with authentic materials, of funeral monuments and Etruscan tombs. The Egyptian Collection is on the first floor. Among the most interesting exhibits: the two statuettes of handmaidens intent on domestic work; the statue of *Thutmosi* III (1490-1436 B.C.); the "Fayyum" portrait of a woman (2nd century A.D.); painted slabs, pillars, sarcophagi, mummies and a war chariot. Also on the first floor, among the Antiquities, Attic *kouroi* of the 6th century B.C.; Etruscan funeral urns; the statue of the *Orator* (c. 100 B.C.); Etruscan sarcophagi; the *Chimaera of Arezzo*; the *Small Idol*; Attic vases and Etruscan *bucchero*.

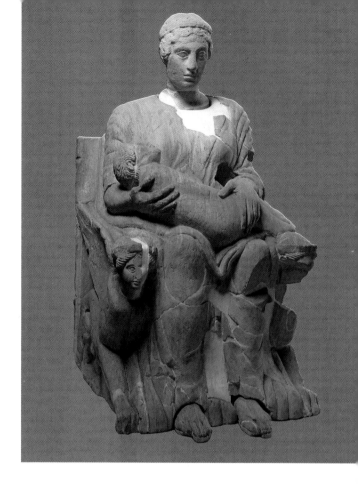

Below: **the François Vase,** a magnificent example of Attic black-figure pottery, signed by the potter *Ergotimos* and the painter *Kleitias.* Right, above: **the Mater Matuta,** an Etruscan sculpture (second half of the 5th cent. B.C.); below: **Attic kouros** (6th cent. B.C.).

145

At the side: **wooden statuette** (Egyptian art, ca 2400 B.C.).

The sculpture represents a maid servant grinding wheat on a stone.

Below, left: **limestone statuette** (Egyptian art, ca 2400 B.C.).

This sculpture depicts a maid servant busy filtering fermented barley for the preparation of beer. Like the preceding wooden figure, this statuette was also placed in a tomb and symbolically guaranteed the deceased the basic provisions in the afterworld.

Below: **Egyptian stele.**

Above: **Chimaera** (4th cent. B.C.).

This masterpiece of Etruscan bronze work depicts the mythical monster with the body and head of a lion, the tail of a serpent and the head of a goat, at the centre of its back, which was killed by Bellerofonte.

At the side: **the sarcophagus of Larthia Seianti** (2nd cent. B.C.).

This work in polychrome terracotta represents Larthia Seianti, a wealthy Etruscan matron, richly dressed and reclining on a kline as she admires herself in a mirror.

The church of San Filippo Neri and the building, seat of the Court, in Piazza San Firenze. At the side: Palazzo del Bargello, seat of the National Museum.

PIAZZA SAN FIRENZE

Not far from Piazza della Signoria, and not very large, this piazza is dominated by two fine, large palaces of different epoch and style. One of these is Palazzo Gondi, by Giuliano da Sangallo (1490-1501). Opposite is the great building of the so-called San Firenze, the best Baroque in Florence, (end of 17th and 18th century). Now the seat of the Tribunal, it incorporates the church of San Filippo Neri, known as San Firenze, with a fine interior, also Baroque.

The **"Prison" of the Bargello,** in a nineteenth-century print.

NATIONAL MUSEUM (BARGELLO)

This is the most important Italian museum of sculpture and minor arts. It is housed in the severe square Bargello palace, a 13th century building of great historical importance, that was begun in 1255 and was first used as the seat of the Captain of the People. After 1574 it was the seat of the Captain of Justice, called the Bargello (that is the chief of police) and the palace became grimly famous for the executions held there; condemned men who escaped capture were hanged in effigy, that is, portraits of them, hanging head downwards, were painted on the city walls; painters engaged on this job included Botticelli, Andrea del Sarto and Andrea del Castagno, known by his contemporaries as Andrea degli Impiccati (Hanged men). The Museum was founded in 1865. A description of the principal works must begin with the splendid courtyard, where, under the arches, is, among other things, a large and very fine cannon of the early 17th century and, among the sculptures, the delightful *Fisherman* by Vincenzo Gemito (1877). One of the rooms on the ground floor contains masterpieces by Michelangelo such as the bust of *Brutus* (c. 1540), who was seen at that time as a heroic liberator from tyranny; the so-called *Pitti tondo* (c. 1504), rendered with the characteristic and expressive "unfinished" style; the *David-Apollo* (c. 1531), delicate and harmonious; the youthful *Drunken Bacchus* (1497-99); among other works, another *Bacchus* by Sansovino (1520) and the bronze bust of *Cosimo I,* by Benvenuto Cellini (1546-57). On the first floor, on the fine balcony are more bronzes by Giambologna, including the famous *Mercury*; in the Donatello Hall, besides masterpieces by the great 15th century sculptor, are numerous terracottas by Luca della Robbia and the panels with the *Sacrifice of Isaac* by Brunelleschi and Ghiberti; in the other rooms, splendid majolicas from Faenza and other factories, enamels, goldsmiths' work, liturgical objects, ivories of various periods. On the second floor: a room with terracottas by Giovanni della Robbia and one with those of Andrea della Robbia; a room devoted to Verrocchio, that also contains works by Rossellino, Pollaiolo and others; lastly, two rooms with the collections of small bronzes and of arms.

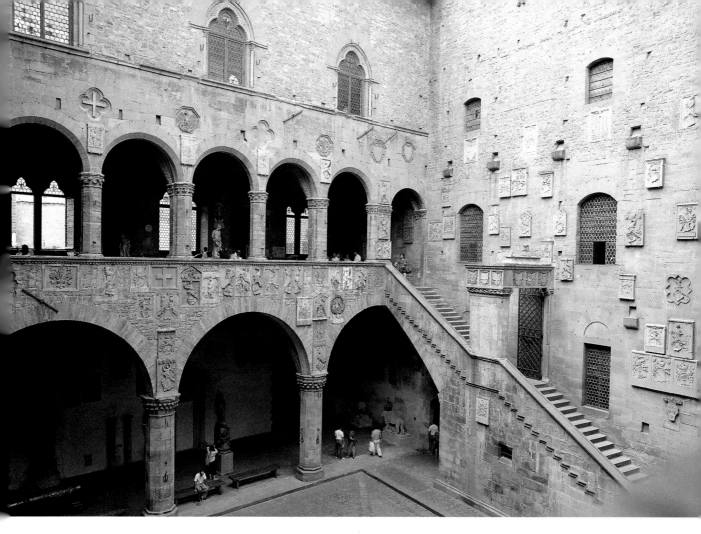

The courtyard and the portico of the Bargello.

Above: **Coronation of Ferdinand I of Aragon (?),** *Florentine school* (15th cent.).

Various attempts have been made in the past to establish who the artist was (Benedetto da Maiano?) and the true identity of the sovereign.

Above, right: **Madonna and Child,** by *Tino di Camaino.*

It almost certainly comes from the tomb of Bishop Orso in the Cathedral of Florence.

At the side: **Madonna and Child between Saints Peter and Paul,** by *Paolo di Giovanni* (1328).

This large group of three statues in pietra serena comes from the outer arch of Porta Romana.

Above: **Narcissus,** by *Benvenuto Cellini* (1565).

Above, left: **Brutus,** by *Michelangelo.*

At the side: **Madonna and Child with the Infant Saint John,** by *Michelangelo,* known as the **"Pitti Tondo"** (ca 1504).
The influence of Leonardo da Vinci's chiaroscuro technique is evident in this tondo which is worked in the characteristic and expressive "non-finito" of Michelangelo.

Following page, from left above: **Cosimo I dei Medici,** by *Benvenuto Cellini* (1545-1547).

Bacchus, by *Michelangelo* (1496).

Mercury, by *Benvenuto Cellini* (1545-1554).
Along with other statuettes, it comes from the base of Cellini's masterpiece, the Perseus.

Perseus, by *Benvenuto Cellini.*
This was probably the trial for the casting of the final statue.

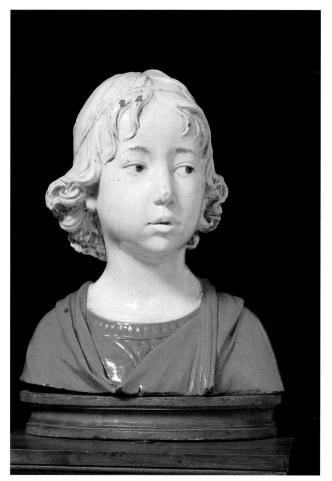

Above: **Madonna and Child,** by *Giovanni della Robbia.*

Above, right: **Idealized Portrait of a Boy,** by *Andrea della Robbia.*

At the side: **Portrait of a young Lady,** by *Andrea della Robbia.*

Preceding page, at the edge: **Saint George,** by *Donatello.*
This lovely marble statue, commissioned by the Armorers' Guild in 1416, was placed in a tabernacle in the church of Orsanmichele.

Above: **David,** by *Donatello* (ca 1430).
Commissioned by Cosimo the Elder, this delightful sculpture in bronze, the first nude made in the Renaissance, comes from the courtyard of the Medici-Riccardi Palace.

Below: **Madonna of the Apple,** by *Luca della Robbia.*
Luca was the founder of this great family of Florentine sculptors and ceramists of the 15th and 16th centuries, famous for the production of their unmistakable glazed terracottas.

155

Above: **Lady Holding Flowers,** by *Verrocchio*.
A lovely marble bust with an almost Leonardesque modelling of the hands.

Above, left: **Francesco Sassetti,** by *Antonio Rossellino*.
The marble bust portrays the wealthy Florentine merchant who commissioned the frescoes for the family chapel in Santa Trinita from Domenico Ghirlandaio in 1485.

At the side: **Madonna and Child with Angels,** by *Antonio Rossellino*.

Facing page: **David,** by *Verrocchio* (ca 1470).
A late work by the great painter and sculptor, this David betrays the influence of Donatello's figure, but the personage is more classical and more detached, as if he were posing in front of his people.

157

The church of Santa Croce on the square of the same name. At the side: **Monument to Dante,** by *Enrico Pazzi* (1865).

Facing page: **the facade of Santa Croce.**

PIAZZA SANTA CROCE

From the Middle Ages onwards this piazza was the scene of festivities, tournaments, meetings, games; there was a famous tournament here between Lorenzo and Giuliano dei Medici, St. Bernardino da Siena preached here, the Florentine Carnival took place here, like the game of football in Renaissance costume. In 1865 Enrico Pazzi placed the monument to Dante (later transferred to the front of the church) in the middle of the square. On the south side of the piazza is Palazzo dell'Antella, whose façade, resting on corbels, was frescoed in the space of three weeks by twenty painters directed by Giuliano da Sangallo (17th century); on the door is a bust of Cosimo II; between two windows on the ground floor is a 16th century marble disc that indicated the central line of the piazza for the football game.

The interior of Santa Croce.

SANTA CROCE

This church originated as a small oratory, built here by a community of monks in 1228. In 1294 Arnolfo di Cambio began the construction of the present basilica, in the monumental but simple form, sober in decoration, that characterises Franciscan churches. Santa Croce was for the Franciscans what Santa Maria Novella, on the other side of the town, was for the Dominicans, the shrine, the core of the order in Florence, the temple par excellence. The church was consecrated in 1443 in the presence of Pope Eugene IV. In 1566 Giorgio Vasari was commissioned by Cosimo I to execute some altars in the side aisles; this involved destroying the old choir and numerous frescoes. The façade of the church was only executed in the mid 19th century from a design by Niccolò Matas, in a neo-Gothic style like the bell-tower, by Gaetano Baccani (1847).

The extraordinary importance of this church, with its numerous works of art, is enhanced by the many tombs of illustrious men (the "urns of the Strong" celebrated by Ugo Foscolo in the *Sepolcri*.) The interior has a nave and two side aisles, with pointed arches resting on octagonal stone pillars. The floor contains no fewer than 276 tombstones, the oldest being 14th century. In the central nave, at the third pillar on the right, is the fine pulpit by Benedetto da Maiano (1472-76); the decorative panels in relief have *Stories of St. Francis*. In the right aisle, at the first pillar, the *Madonna of the Milk* by Rossellino (1478); opposite, the funeral monument to Michelangelo by Vasari and helpers (1570); the sculptures are allegories of Painting, Sculpture and Architecture. There are also the Cenotaph of Dante Alighieri (buried at Ravenna) by Stefano Ricci (1829);

Above: **Pulpit,** by *Benedetto da Maiano* (15th cent.).
Above, right: **Annunciation,** by *Donatello* (1436). At
the side: **Madonna "del Latte",** by *Antonio Rossellino.*

the tomb of Vittorio Alfieri, executed by Canova in
1810; that of Niccolò Machiavelli, by Spinazzi (1787);
the splendid *Annunciation* by Donatello (c. 1435); the
monument to Leonardo Bruni, by Rossellino (c. 1444);
the tombs of Gioacchino Rossini and Ugo Foscolo. In
the right transept, on the right, is the Castellani chapel,
frescoed about 1385 by Agnolo Gaddi with *Stories of St.
Nicholas of Bari, John the Baptist,* and *Anthony Abbot.*
At the end of the transept is the entrance to the
Baroncelli Chapel, frescoed with *Stories of the Virgin* by
Taddeo Gaddi; on the altar a polyptych with the
Coronation of the Virgin, from the workshop of Giotto.
At the corner of the transept is the entrance to the fine
14th century Sacristy; on the right wall, three episodes
from the *Passion* by Taddeo Gaddi and others; in the
end wall is the entrance to the Rinuccini Chapel, with

frescoes by Giovanni da Milano. Returning to the church one should visit the series of chapels along the end; the Peruzzi Chapel (fourth from the right) has splendid frescoes by Giotto with *Stories of the Baptist* and *St. John the Evangelist*; the Bardi Chapel (the fifth) has *Stories of St. Francis*, also by Giotto; this cycle is to be placed among the painter's masterpieces (c. 1325); the Chapel of the High Altar has frescoes by Agnolo Gaddi and a polyptych by Niccolò Gerini (end of 14th century). Of the end chapels on the left, the Bardi di Vernio Chapel has fine *Stories of St. Sylvester*, by Maso di Banco (c. 1340). The Bardi Chapel at the end of the transept has a *Crucifix* by Donatello (c. 1425). On the left, the Salviati Chapel with the 19th century tomb of Sofia Zamoyski by Lorenzo Bartolini. In the left aisle, another series of funeral monuments; among others, the tomb of Galileo Galilei by Giulio Foggini (18th century).

At the side: **Tomb of Michelangelo** designed by *Vasari* (1570). Below, from left to right: **Monument to Galileo Galilei,** by *Giulio Foggini* (1737); **cenotaph to Dante,** by *Stefano Ricci* (1829).

Facing page: **the Sanctuary,** completely frescoed by *Agnolo Gaddi* with the Legend of the Cross.

At the side: **the Sacristy** with the frescoes by *Taddeo Gaddi, Spinello Aretino* and *Niccolo Gerini.* Below, left to right: **Crucifixion,** by *Taddeo Gaddi*; **Madonna and Child with Saints**, by *Giovanni del Biondo* (1379), on the altar of the Rinuccini Chapel.

Preceding page, above, left: **the Bardi Chapel and the Peruzzi Chapel.** Right: **Saint Francis and Events from his Life,** *anonymous Florentine artist* (13th cent.). Below: **The Funeral of Saint Francis,** by *Giotto,* in the Bardi Chapel.

The entrance portico of the Pazzi Chapel.

PAZZI CHAPEL

On the right of the church of Santa Croce are the buildings of the Franciscan monastery. The first Cloister is against the wall of the right aisle; the porticoes are 14th-15th century; on the right of the entrance is the monument to Florence Nightingale, (1820-1910), the heroic "Lady of the Lamp" who anticipated the work of the Red Cross on the battlefields and in the field hospitals during the Crimean War. At the end of the cloister appears the wonderful front of the Pazzi chapel. Filippo Brunelleschi designed the building and began it (it had the function of chapterhouse of the monastery and family burial chapel for the commissioners) about 1430; he worked on it at intervals until 1444, then other architects completed the building. A pronaos precedes the entrance; this has six Corinthian columns and a wide central arch between elegant inset panels in pietra serena; the frieze with *heads of cherubs* is by Desiderio da Settignano. The chapel has a cupola with conical covering (1461) and under the portico is another small cupola in coloured terracotta, by Luca della Robbia; by the same, the Tondo of St. Andrew over the door, the panels of which are splendidly carved by Giuliano da Maiano (1472). The rectangular interior has the geometrical limpidity and measured rhythm of the best creations of Brunelleschi: white walls, grooved pilaster strips in pietra serena, wide arches; the only touches of colour are the fine tondi by Luca della Robbia, with figures of *Apostles* and *Evangelists*. In the presbytery, a stained glass panel attributed to Alesso Baldovinetti and a small cupola with Signs of the Zodiac. Going out into the First Cloister, a doorway on the left leads into the Large Cloister, designed by Brunelleschi.

Interior of the Pazzi Chapel. Below, left: **the cupola;** right: **ceramic tondo depicting an apostle,** by *Luca della Robbia.*

Crucifix, by *Cimabue* (1280). At the side: **Saint Louis,** bronze statue, by *Donatello* (1423). Below: **Della Robbia tabernacle.**

SANTA CROCE MUSEUM

This is housed in some of the rooms of the Monastery of Santa Croce. The first, and most important of these is the old 14th century Refectory; the end wall is covered by an enormous fresco by Taddeo Gaddi representing the *Tree of Life*, the *Last Supper* and other scenes; on the right wall is the grandiose *Crucifix* painted on wood by Cimabue, badly damaged by the flooding in 1966, and three fragments of the *Triumph of Death* frescoed by Orcagna on the walls of Santa Croce (they were found under Vasari's altars, and detached); on the left is the *St. Ludovic* in bronze by Donatello (1423). The remains of fourteenth and fifteenth century glass windows, the work of Andrea del Castagno, Agnolo Bronzino, Giorgio Vasari and others, are kept in the other rooms.

HORNE MUSEUM

At the beginning of this century Herbert Percy Horne gathered together a fine collection of furniture, pictures, sculptures and other objects, in a beautiful 15th century palace in Via dei Benci that belonged to the Alberti family. Among the principal works, which the English collector donated to the Italian State, are: a stucco *Madonna* by Antonio Rossellino; a fine *Holy Family* by Beccafumi; the splendid early 15th century inlaid sacristy bench; *Madonna and Saints* by Lorenzo Monaco; the *Allegory of Music* by Dosso Dossi; a *Madonna* and a *Pietà* both attributed to Simone Martini; the fragment of a polyptych by Pietro Lorenzetti; the magnificent *St. Stephen* by Giotto; the figure of *Esther* by Filippino Lippi: the fragment of a *story of St. Julian* by Masaccio; drawings, coins, majolicas and cutlery.

Right: **Saint Stephen,** by *Giotto* (Horne Museum).
Below: **Queen Vasti,** by *Filippino Lippi* (Bardini Museum).

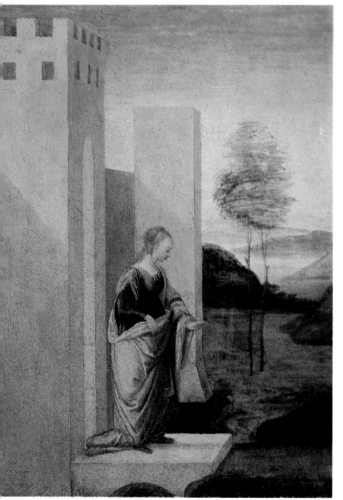

BARDINI MUSEUM

This collection, constituted at the beginning of this century by the antiquarian Stefano Bardini, is housed in the fine 19th century Bardini Palace in Piazza dei Mozzi, (opposite the historic Ponte alle Grazie, that goes back to 1237, but was rebuilt after World War II) left to the Comune of Florence in 1923. The museum still has the character of a rich private collection; the rooms are full of furniture, paintings, sculpture, weapons, tapestries and works of art and craftsmanship of various periods and origins. Among the principal works are a *Madonna and Child* attributed to Lucas Cranach the Elder; *Charity*, by Tino di Camaino (early 14th century); splendid 16th-17th century Persian carpets; a bas-relief of the Virgin and Child with Angels, attributed to Donatello; a series of 15th century chests; a fine *St. Michael the Archangel* by Antonio del Pollaiolo. On the second floor of the palace is the interesting Corsi gallery, a collection of works of art ranging from the twelfth to the nineteenth century.

CASA BUONARROTI

This is a fine 15th century palace at N° 70 Via Ghibellina. It is not, however, the birthplace of Michelangelo; he was born to a noble family of Florentine origin on March 6th 1475 at Caprese, in the Casentino district; his father had been sent there to act as mayor. The house in Florence was bought by Michelangelo, who never lived there, for his nephew Leonardo, who was to be involved in a sensational episode. The great artist went to Rome and after some time died there on February 18th 1564; he was buried in the church of the Holy Apostles. A few days after the funeral Leonardo Buonarroti, in agreement with Cosimo I dei Medici, managed to recover his body and bring it in secret to Florence, where another solemn funeral was celebrated on July 14th. Subsequently Michelangelo Buonarroti the Younger, the artist's great nephew and a distinguished man of letters, had some rooms in the house decorated, for this purpose commissioning some of the best known painters in early 17th century Florence, including Giovanni da San Giovanni, Empoli, Matteo Rosselli, Francesco Furini and Artemisia Gentileschi, to paint scenes of the glorification of Michelangelo. The palace belonged to the Buonarroti family until 1858, when Cosimo, the last direct descendant of the family, ceded it to the State. The numerous rooms contain many works by Michelangelo, including the first works by the sculptor and also drawings, models and sketches. Among works by other artists, besides copies of those by Michelangelo and portraits of members of the Buonarroti family, there is a notable predella with *Stories of St. Nicholas of Bari*, by Giovanni di Francesco, (15th century) a *Narcissus* attributed to Paolo Uccello, and a *Love Scene*, an early work by Titian.

Above: **Study for Porta Pia in Rome,** by *Michelangelo.* Below: **A Miracle of Saint Nicolas of Bari,** by *Giovanni di Francesco* (15th cent.).

The Last Supper, by *Andrea del Sarto* and **detail**
(Cenacolo di San Salvi).

LAST SUPPERS

In old monasteries the Refectory was usually frescoed with the scene of the Last Supper. The iconography stayed unchanged for centuries and consisted of a long table with Christ and His Apostles seen from the front, and only Judas sometimes sitting on the other side. There are many examples of this preserved in Florence: among the oldest, that by Taddeo Gaddi in Santa Croce and that by Orcagna in Santo Spirito. Among those of the 15th century there is a beautiful *Last Supper* by Andrea del Castagno in Santa Apollonia (Via XXVII Aprile, N° 1) of harsh severe realism (1447). At the end of the century, while Perugino was painting the quiet tranquil *Last Supper* in the Conservatorio di Foligno (Via Faenza N° 42) Domenico Ghirlandaio executed no fewer than four *Suppers*, the best and most famous being that at Ognissanti (1480). Lastly, Andrea del Sarto painted the last Florentine masterpiece of the kind, the Last Supper of San Salvi (Via A. del Sarto N° 16). The "faultless painter" as Vasari called him here shows his great instinct for colour, finesse of draughstmanship and expressive natural gift.

Interior of the Synagogue. Preceding page: **the facade.**

THE SYNAGOGUE

This marvellous temple, so prized by the Jewish community of Florence, was commenced in 1874 and was designed by the architects Treves, Falcini and Micheli. It was inaugurated on the 24th October 1882, after eight years of hard work. The construction of the monumental building was financed by a conspicuous fund bequeathed by David Levi, who had been the chairman of the Board of the Israelitic University of Florence from 1860 to 1870. The building is in pure Moorish style. The interior is completely frescoed, while the Ehal is covered with gleaming Venetian mosaic. Due to the predominatly Levantine Jewish origin of the Florentine community, the official rite is orthodox Sephardic, whilst the Ashkenazi minority meets in a room next-door to the Temple. The Synagogue was much damaged during the IInd World War and suffered further during the 1966 flood. The restoration has been carried out thanks to the contributions of the many visitors.

Monument to Michelangelo at the centre of Piazzale Michelangelo.

PIAZZALE MICHELANGELO

On the south side of the Arno, going along Viale Michelangelo or else walking up the ramps that go up from the San Niccolò gate, one comes to a large panoramic terrace, which affords a view over the whole town and the surrounding hills: Piazzale Michelangelo. This large area was conceived by Giuseppe Poggi in the 1860's as the scenographic climax to his work of "redesigning" the town; Florence was then the capital of Italy. In the centre of the square is the monument to Michelangelo erected in 1875 with copies in bronze of some of his marble statues. Going on up the hill, behind Piazzale Michelangelo, is the beautiful little church of San Salvatore al Monte, begun by Cronaca in 1495. Inside there appears for the first time in the Renaissance a double order of columns, superimposed; and there are still some works of the 16th century.

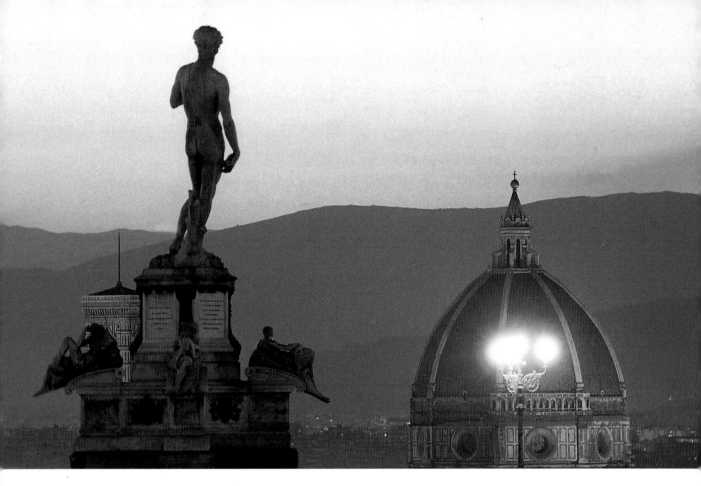

Two views of Piazzale Michelangelo. On the following pages: **panorama of the city from the Piazzale.**

175

San Miniato al Monte. On the facing page: **interior**.

SAN MINIATO AL MONTE

One of the oldest and most beautiful churches in Florence, it stands on the site of the first Christian settlements in the city, the old *Mons Florentinus*, where the woods were full, first of catacombs, then of oratories and the little hovels of monks. One oratory was dedicated to San Miniato, who suffered martyrdom on the hill in the 4th century, and the Romanesque church was built over this in the 11th-13th century. The façade is covered with marble in two colours, in a clear, solemn design; the fine mosaic in the centre (13th century, much restored) represents *Christ between the Virgin and St. Miniato*; at the top of the tympanum, *the Eagle*, the symbol of the Guild of Woolmerchants whose task it was to organize the upkeep of the church. The interior has a nave and two side aisles, with a crypt and a raised presbytery above it; the floor of the nave is set with splendid slabs of inlaid marble. In the centre, between the two flights of steps leading up to the presbytery, is the Crucifix Chapel, by Michelozzo (1448), commissioned by Piero the Gouty, the father of

Lorenzo the Magnificent. The chapel was built to house a famous Crucifix which miraculously nodded to St. Giovanni Gualberto and is now in Santa Trinita; the vault has coffers by Luca della Robbia; on the end wall, panels painted by Angolo Gaddi. From the left aisle one enters the Chapel of the Cardinal of Portugal, one of the most elegant creations of the Florentine Renaissance, by Antonio Manetti (1461-66) a pupil of Brunelleschi; this contains the tomb of Jacopo Di Lusitania, archbishop of Lisbon, by Rossellino; fine della Robbia terracottas on the vault, a splendid *Annunciation* by Baldovinetti (on the left) and two *angels* frescoed by Antonio and Piero del Pollaiolo (on the wall at the end, above the copy of the *Saints Eustace, James and Vincent* by Antonio and Piero, which is now at the Uffizi). On the vault of the crypt, above the altar, are frescoes of *Saints and Prophets* by Taddeo Gaddi. The presbytery of the church is surrounded with fine 13th century marble parapets on which is the elegant pulpit; on the right altar is a painting on wood by Jacopo del Casentino with

St. Miniato and eight scenes of his life; the mosaic in the apse represents *Christ enthroned between the Virgin, St. Miniato and the symbols of the Evangelists* (1279, but restored in 1491 by Baldovinetti). From the Presbytery one goes on the right to the Sacristy, frescoed after 1387 by Spinello Aretino, with *Stories of St. Benedict*; the door next to that of the Sacristy leads into the Cloister, with the remains of frescoes by Andrea del Castagno and, in the loggia above, by Paolo Uccello. On the right of the church is the Bishops' Palace (13th-14th century). Round the church are the walls of the Fortress erected by Michelangelo in 1529 to defend Florence during the siege by the Imperial troops.

At the side: **The Chapel of the Crucifix,** commissioned by Piero the Gouty from *Michelozzo,* in 1488. Below, left: **the Tomb of Jacopo di Lusitania,** archbishop of Lisbon, by *Antonio Rossellino.* Below: **the crypt,** frescoed by *Taddeo Gaddi.*

Christ Enthroned between the Virgin and Saint Minias with the Symbols of the Evangelists (1297).

This vigorous mosaic, in the conch of the apse, was restored by Baldovinetti in 1491.

At the side: **Events from the Life of Saint Benedict,** by *Spinello Aretino* (detail).

Forte Belvedere.

FORT BELVEDERE

Perched on the top of the hill of St. George, the fort is the highest point in Florence, and the splendid views one enjoys from its parapets in all directions fully justify the Fort's name of Belvedere (beautiful view). Already envisaged as a fort in the Duke of Athens' time, before his expulsion from Florence, it was finally commenced in 1590, by order of Ferdinand Ist de' Medici, to designs by the famous military engineer, Bernardo Buontalenti. The Fort was designed to defend the city from the South and to protect the grand-ducal family in times of civil unrest. The governor of the Fort's residence is, at present, used for internationally renowned exhibitions.

THE GATES OF FLORENCE

The third and last circle of walls was built around 1300, after the earlier Roman brick walls had been enlarged on various occasions. The third circle was amply sufficient until 1865, when the town was extensively restructured, a number of Medieval gates demolished and the centre of the town gutted to create space for new religious and civilian buildings. Among the numerous gates still standing, are the *Porta Sangallo*, the *Porta alla Croce*, both dating back to 1284; *Porta Romana*, south of the town, which still preserves its ancient oakwood, nail-studded gates and *Porta San Giorgio*, dating back to 1260, very well preserved.

Porta alla Croce.

Porta Romana.

Porta Sangallo.

Porta San Giorgio.

The Certosa of Galluzzo. Below: the church of the Certosa.

CHARTERHOUSE OF GALLUZZO

Built as a mediaeval castle, the Charterhouse is in a fine position on the Hill of Montaguto, near Galluzzo, about 3 miles away from Florence. Its construction began in 1341 by order of the Florentine condottiere and statesman Niccolò Acciaiuoli; work on it continued during later centuries and the monastery was enriched with works of art. Some of the rooms are used as an Art Gallery; among the most interesting works are the five large lunettes frescoed by Pontormo in one of the cloisters of the Charterhouse between 1523 and 1525 (detached and restored) representing the *Prayer in the Garden*, *Jesus and Pilate*, the *Ascent to Calvary*, the *Descent from the Cross* and the *Resurrection*. The church of the Certosa, dedicated to San Lorenzo, is a work of the 16th century, perhaps by Fancelli; on the right side is a series of chapels, which include the fine 16th century chapel of Santa Maria and the underground chapels of Sant'Andrea (with the 16th century tomb of Cardinal Agnolo II Acciaiuoli, perhaps by Francesco da Sangallo) and of Tobias, with remarkable Acciaiuoli tombs; there is an interesting Monks' Choir, with carved sixteenth century choirstalls.

Wooden choirstalls. Below, left: **Madonna and Child,** by *Lucas Cranach.* Right: **Jesus before Pilate**, by *Pontormo.*

The hills of Fiesole

FIESOLE

A charming little town about 4 miles north of Florence, it was founded by the Etruscans in the 4th century B.C.; three centuries later it was conquered by the Romans. After the fall of the Empire it was an important bishopric; in the 12th century it succumbed to its stronger neighbour, Florence. Having lost all its political power, it came to be, with time, a favourite summer resort for rich Florentines (also the Medicis had a villa there) and, in the 19th century, also for foreign visitors, especially the English. The centre of the little town is Piazza Mino, where the principal public buildings are. The Cathedral was erected in 1028 and later enlarged in 1256 and 1300; in the Salutati Chapel are frescoes by Cosimo Rosselli and the tomb of Bishop Leonardo Salutati, by Mino da Fiesole, 15th century; on the High Altar is a triptych by Bicci di Lorenzo (c. 1440); in the crypt, which is Romanesque, are 15th century frescoes by Benedetto di Nanni, a baptismal font by Francesco del Tadda (16th century) and the wooden Bishop's Chair by Andrea Corsini (14th century). The Bandini Museum nearby has interesting Della Robbia terracottas and works by Agnolo and Taddeo Gaddi, Lorenzo Monaco and Jacopo del Sellaio. Also in Piazza Mino is the Praetorian Palace (15th century) with façade and loggia covered with coats of arms. Near the piazza is the Roman theatre (1st century B.C.) which seats an audience of 3000 and is still in use for summer concerts and other performances. In the vicinity of the theatre are the remains of a temple (first Etruscan and later Roman) and some Roman baths. The Archaeological Museum beside the area of excavation contains relics of Etruscan and Roman Fiesole; urns from Chiusi and Volterra; storied stelae, typical of the zone; Greek vases, objects in *bucchero*, small bronzes. Returning to the piazza, one goes up a very steep little road to Sant'Alessandro, an ancient church standing on the site of an Etruscan temple. A little beyond it are the church and monastery of San Francesco; this church was built between the 14th and 15th century, and has a simple façade with a rose-window and suspended porch. The interior is Gothic with a single nave; the High Altar has a beautiful *Annunciation* by Raffaellino del Garbo (early 16th century); at the second altar on the left, *Madonna and Saints* by the school of Perugino; next to it, a *Conception* by Cosimo Rosselli; a fine early 16th century inlaid choir. On the right of the church is the small Cloister of St. Bernardino (13th-14th century). Half way between Fiesole and Florence is the church of San Domenico, built in the 15th century but restored in the 17th; it contains a *Madonna and Child with Angels and Saints* by Fra Angelico (c. 1430) who was prior of the nearby monastery. Via di Badia dei Roccettini goes

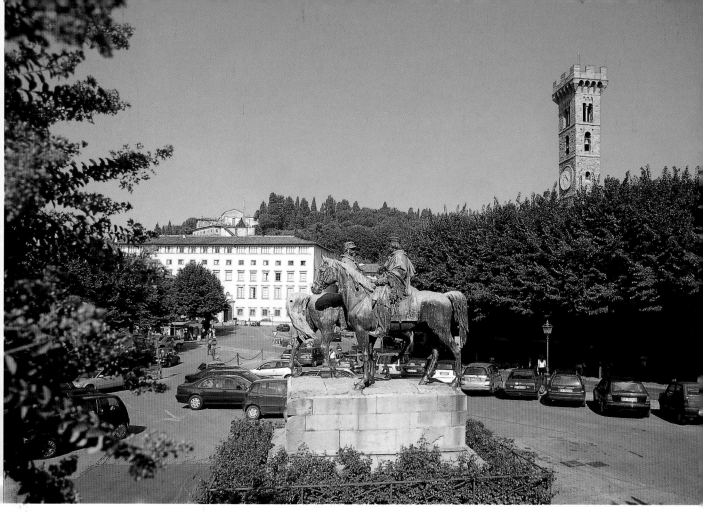

Piazza Mino da Fiesole. Below: the church of San Francesco.

The road that leads to San Francesco, on the hill of the same name. Below: **the Roman theatre** (1st cent. B.C.).

down from San Domenico to the Badia Fiesolana. The Cathedral of Fiesole in the early Middle Ages, the church was restored by the Camaldolese monks in the 11th century, after it had been abandoned; the small, magnificent Romanesque façade belongs to this period. In 1456 the interior was restored on behalf of Cosimo the Elder, who lived here, and here assembled part of his collection of manuscripts, now kept in the Laurentian Library. The monastery, rebuilt several times, changed functions periodically: in 1529-30 it was the Spanish headquarters in the siege of the city; in 1631 a hospital for those stricken with the plague; in 1753 the seat of the Accademia dei Georgofili (the first agricultural academy in Europe); then of a polygraphic institute, of a private school run by the Scolopian monks, and now of the European University.

At the side: **Etruscan sepulchral stele** (5th cent. B.C.). (Archaeological Museum of Fiesole).
A banquet and a funeral dance are depicted.

Below, right: **torso of a woman.** Left: **torso of a man,** both works dating to Roman times (Archaeological Museum of Fiesole).

p.ta
al Prato

v. della Scala

v. Alamanni

STAZ. F.S.
S. MARIA NOVELLA

p.za
Adua

Mercato
Centr.

v. Nazionale

v. dell'Ariento

v. Faenza

il Prato

v. Orti
Oricellari

v. della Scala

p.za
Stazione

S. Maria
Novella

p.za
Unità

Cappelle
Medicee

S. Lorenzo

v. Panzani

Biblioteca
Laurenziana

Pal.
Favard

v. Palazzuolo

b.go Ognissanti

Ognissanti

p.za
S. Maria
Novella

v. Cerretani

v.d.Pecori

lungarno Vespucci

p.za
Ognissanti

Osp.
S. Giovanni
di Dio

v. de' Fossi

Pal.
Strozzi

p.za
Repubb

p.te Vespucci

F. Arno

p.za
Goldoni

v. Vigna Nuova

Pal.
Corsini

v. Tornabuoni

Pal. A
d. Lan

p.ta
Frediano

lung. Soderini

p.za
Cestello

b.go S. Frediano

p.te alla

Carraia

lung. Corsini

S. Trinita

v. Porta Rossa

Log
de
Porcell

S.
Frediano

v. del Leone

lung. Guicciardini

v. S. Spirito

p.te

S. Trinita

lung. Acciaioli

b.go SS. Apostoli

F. Arno

b.go S. Jacopo

Ponte

Vecchio

p.za del
Carmine

v. del Serragli

S. Maria
d. Carmine

S. Spirito

v. Maggio

v. Guicciardini

S. Felicita

p.za Tasso

v. della Chiesa

p.za Pitti

Pal. Pitti

v.le Petrarca

Giardino
Torrigiani

La Specola
(Mus. Zool.)

v. Romana

Giardino di Boboli

Forte Belved